MIDLAND RED
in NBC Days

MIKE GREENWOOD and PAUL ROBERTS

Ian Allan PUBLISHING

First published 2014

ISBN 978 0 7110 3717 5

Published by Ian Allan Publishing

an imprint of Ian Allan Publishing Ltd, Hersham, Surrey
KT12 4RG.

Printed in Bulgaria.

Visit the Ian Allan Publishing website at
www.ianallanpublishing.com

Picture Credits

Every effort has been made to identify and correctly
attribute photographic credits. Should any error have
occurred this is entirely unintentional.

FRONT COVER D9 No 5434 was an early recipient of NBC
poppy red livery. The bus is operating a local Leamington Spa
town service, and is passing the Royal Pump Rooms and Baths
in the Parade. Tom Moore

BACK COVER Making quite a sight on 19 April 1987, this convoy
of seven Midland Fox ECW-bodied Leyland Olympians is heading
along the A6 towards Loughborough. Derek Bailey collection

TITLE PAGE NBC have stamped their authority on all three
Midland Red buses in this March 1979 view. D9 No 5370
threads its way into Leicester St Margaret's bus station
driving between a Leyland Leopard and a Leyland National
whilst the preoccupied inspector relies on the skills of the
driver to avoid being run over. Mike Greenwood

RIGHT BMMO S17 No 5729 of 1966 loads up with passengers
under a cloudless sky at Nuneaton bus station in June 1975.
Alongside is S23 No 5936, built in 1969; also visible are an
N2-class Leyland National and a BMMO D9 double-decker.
Tom Moore

CONTENTS

INTRODUCTION

The authors have found the subject of this book fascinating, although, given that both are keen enthusiasts of Midland Red, chronicling the company's demise from its once-great status has been a rather sobering experience. However, the NBC era is one that many enthusiasts will actually remember with fondness, and it is undoubtedly important that the final stage of the company's long and illustrious history should receive appropriate attention.

Midland 'Red' had started life in 1904 with the grandiose title of 'The Birmingham & Midland Motor Omnibus Company Ltd'. Whilst the fleetname 'MIDLAND' was displayed on the sides of buses it was the combination of this with the red livery that resulted in the name that was commonly used as a reference to the company.

Over the course of the next few decades the company grew from being a horse-bus operator on the west side of Birmingham to a provider of motor-bus services in 18 counties in England and Wales. In the years following World War 2 staff and enthusiasts all recognised the company, known by its initials BMMO, not only as an operator of bus and coach services but also as a builder of quality vehicles to operate on their routes. The public readily identified

with the name 'Midland Red', which was used in timetables and publicity material, although it took until 1974 for this to become the official company name. Only then, after legislation had resulted in the transfer of 119 services to the West Midlands Passenger Transport Executive, was the company officially renamed 'Midland Red Omnibus Co Ltd', reflecting the name that had been in common usage for many decades previously.

It is, however, some years before 1974 that our story begins. On 1 January 1969, as a result of the Transport Act 1968, the Transport Holding Co's interests came under the ownership of the newly formed National Bus Company. NBC started with a fleet of more than 20,000 vehicles operating throughout England and Wales. Midland Red had been part of the vast British Electric Traction (BET) empire, but the group sold its UK bus interests to the state-owned Transport Holding Co (THC) on 14 March 1968. With a fleet of 1,769 vehicles it was, at the time NBC assumed control, the largest of the THC companies. That the Midland Red fleet would dwindle to less than half this size by the early 1980s was a sign of its changing fortunes. This was partly as a result of the formation of the West Midlands Passenger Transport Executive, another child of the

ABOVE This scene, recorded a year after Midland Red had become part of the National Bus Company, will gladden the hearts of BMMO enthusiasts – but it was not to last! Six of the eight double-deck buses are of BMMO manufacture – five D9s dating from the 1960s and a D7 from the 1950s. They are loading or resting under the ever-watchful eye of Dudley Castle. The two Daimler Fleetlines are a sign of modern times, but there is nothing to show that Midland Red was now part of NBC; in fact nothing has changed since BET days, and there is no hint of the upheaval to come. Within four years West Midlands PTE would operate all of the services in Dudley, as a result of which many of the buses visible would don a new coat of blue and cream, but Midland Red buses would continue to serve the surrounding counties for many years to come. Stuart Turner

1968 Act, and partly through further reorganisations and divisions within Midland Red as the business re-shaped itself to cope with falling patronage.

In 1973 the takeover by WMPTE of all those Midland Red routes wholly within its area became a financial time-bomb for the company. This immediately resulted in the fleet strength being reduced by 413 vehicles as most of the Black Country and Birmingham garages were transferred to the PTE. Some small redress was made soon afterwards when Midland Red purchased a number of independent operators in Staffordshire and Shropshire. These were Coopers of Oakengates, with 13 vehicles, and Green Bus of Rugeley, with 29 vehicles. The following year the five-vehicle fleet of Hoggins of Wrockwardine Wood was acquired, and 50 buses and coaches came with the purchase of Harper Bros (Heath Hayes) Ltd, although not all of these entered service with Midland Red.

A major cull of routes and vehicles began in 1976 as part of the Viable Network Project, which soon evolved into the Market Analysis Project. This involved passenger surveys on all routes, and then adjustments to the network, which were sometimes drastic, would follow.

More changes occurred as local branding was added to the corporate livery, starting with 'Reddibus' in March 1976. Further local networks and names were introduced as a result of VNP/MAP, and these eventually covered more than a dozen operating areas within the company territory. However, these changes were insufficient to arrest the decline in company' fortunes, and in 1981 the decision was taken to divide its operations. With effect from 6 September bus services were provided by four regional operating companies – Midland Red (North) Ltd, Midland Red (South) Ltd, Midland Red (East) Ltd and Midland Red (West) Ltd – and the majority of long-distance coaching

operations by Midland Red (Express) Ltd, while Midland Red Omnibus Co Ltd, no longer a bus-operating company, remained in control of Carlyle Works. The thinking behind this was that each of the regional operating companies could then provide its own network based on commercial viability plus whatever additional funding the relevant local authorities in its particular region was willing to provide.

The final phase of the story came with the sell-off of the six new companies, beginning with Midland Red (West) and Midland Red Coaches – formerly Midland Red (Express) – in December 1986 and ending with Midland Red (North) in January 1988.

The authors are grateful to those Midland Red enthusiasts who have provided invaluable guidance in compiling the text and to the photographers whose work, mostly hitherto unpublished, illustrates so comprehensively this final part of the Midland Red story.

Mike Greenwood
Paul Roberts
Leicester
November 2013

BELOW The regular Staff Bulletin clearly represented the General Manager's feelings on the subject of nationalisation.

Midland Red NBC Timeline

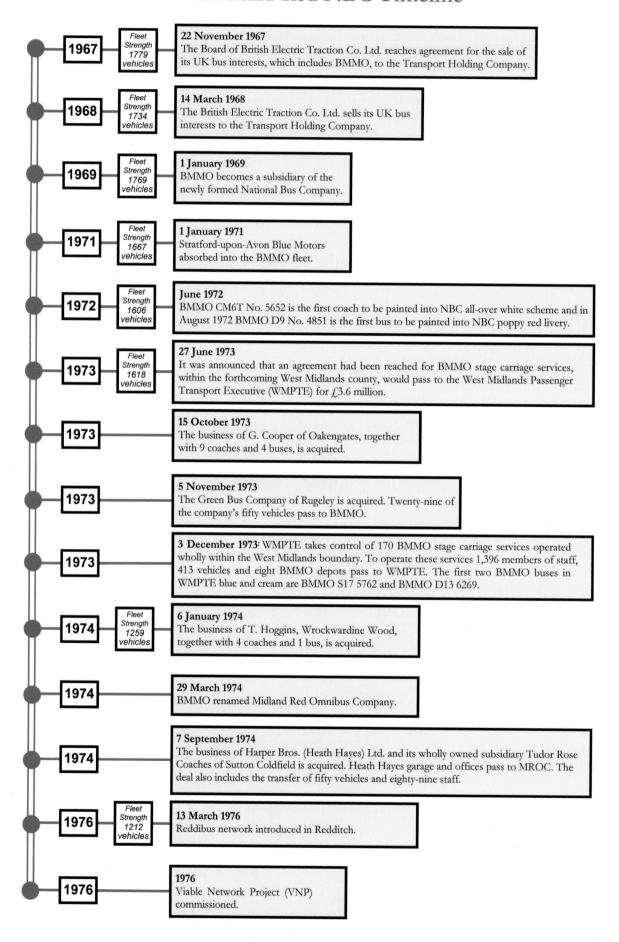

1967 · *Fleet Strength 1779 vehicles*

22 November 1967
The Board of British Electric Traction Co. Ltd. reaches agreement for the sale of its UK bus interests, which includes BMMO, to the Transport Holding Company.

1968 · *Fleet Strength 1734 vehicles*

14 March 1968
The British Electric Traction Co. Ltd. sells its UK bus interests to the Transport Holding Company.

1969 · *Fleet Strength 1769 vehicles*

1 January 1969
BMMO becomes a subsidiary of the newly formed National Bus Company.

1971 · *Fleet Strength 1667 vehicles*

1 January 1971
Stratford-upon-Avon Blue Motors absorbed into the BMMO fleet.

1972 · *Fleet Strength 1606 vehicles*

June 1972
BMMO CM6T No. 5652 is the first coach to be painted into NBC all-over white scheme and in August 1972 BMMO D9 No. 4851 is the first bus to be painted into NBC poppy red livery.

1973 · *Fleet Strength 1618 vehicles*

27 June 1973
It was announced that an agreement had been reached for BMMO stage carriage services, within the forthcoming West Midlands county, would pass to the West Midlands Passenger Transport Executive (WMPTE) for £3.6 million.

1973

15 October 1973
The business of G. Cooper of Oakengates, together with 9 coaches and 4 buses, is acquired.

1973

5 November 1973
The Green Bus Company of Rugeley is acquired. Twenty-nine of the company's fifty vehicles pass to BMMO.

1973

3 December 1973: WMPTE takes control of 170 BMMO stage carriage services operated wholly within the West Midlands boundary. To operate these services 1,396 members of staff, 413 vehicles and eight BMMO depots pass to WMPTE. The first two BMMO buses in WMPTE blue and cream are BMMO S17 5762 and BMMO D13 6269.

1974 · *Fleet Strength 1259 vehicles*

6 January 1974
The business of T. Hoggins, Wrockwardine Wood, together with 4 coaches and 1 bus, is acquired.

1974

29 March 1974
BMMO renamed Midland Red Omnibus Company.

1974

7 September 1974
The business of Harper Bros. (Heath Hayes) Ltd. and its wholly owned subsidiary Tudor Rose Coaches of Sutton Coldfield is acquired. Heath Hayes garage and offices pass to MROC. The deal also includes the transfer of fifty vehicles and eighty-nine staff.

1976 · *Fleet Strength 1212 vehicles*

13 March 1976
Reddibus network introduced in Redditch.

1976

1976
Viable Network Project (VNP) commissioned.

Midland Red NBC Timeline

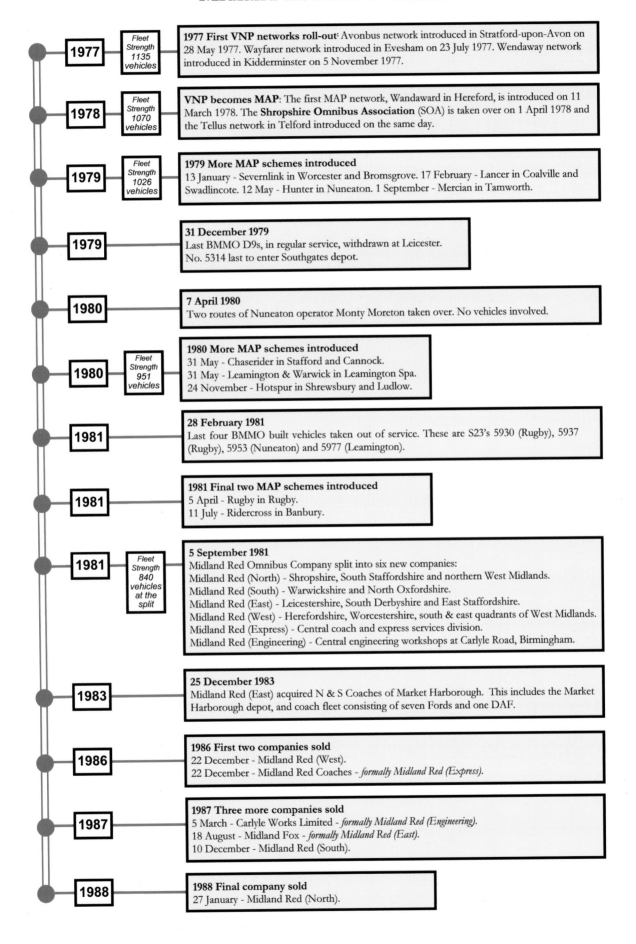

1977

Fleet Strength 1135 vehicles

1977 First VNP networks roll-out: Avonbus network introduced in Stratford-upon-Avon on 28 May 1977. Wayfarer network introduced in Evesham on 23 July 1977. Wendaway network introduced in Kidderminster on 5 November 1977.

1978

Fleet Strength 1070 vehicles

VNP becomes MAP: The first MAP network, Wandaward in Hereford, is introduced on 11 March 1978. The **Shropshire Omnibus Association** (SOA) is taken over on 1 April 1978 and the Tellus network in Telford introduced on the same day.

1979

Fleet Strength 1026 vehicles

1979 More MAP schemes introduced
13 January - Severnlink in Worcester and Bromsgrove. 17 February - Lancer in Coalville and Swadlincote. 12 May - Hunter in Nuneaton. 1 September - Mercian in Tamworth.

1979

31 December 1979
Last BMMO D9s, in regular service, withdrawn at Leicester.
No. 5314 last to enter Southgates depot.

1980

7 April 1980
Two routes of Nuneaton operator Monty Moreton taken over. No vehicles involved.

1980

Fleet Strength 951 vehicles

1980 More MAP schemes introduced
31 May - Chaserider in Stafford and Cannock.
31 May - Leamington & Warwick in Leamington Spa.
24 November - Hotspur in Shrewsbury and Ludlow.

1981

28 February 1981
Last four BMMO built vehicles taken out of service. These are S23's 5930 (Rugby), 5937 (Rugby), 5953 (Nuneaton) and 5977 (Leamington).

1981

1981 Final two MAP schemes introduced
5 April - Rugby in Rugby.
11 July - Ridercross in Banbury.

1981

Fleet Strength 840 vehicles at the split

5 September 1981
Midland Red Omnibus Company split into six new companies:
Midland Red (North) - Shropshire, South Staffordshire and northern West Midlands.
Midland Red (South) - Warwickshire and North Oxfordshire.
Midland Red (East) - Leicestershire, South Derbyshire and East Staffordshire.
Midland Red (West) - Herefordshire, Worcestershire, south & east quadrants of West Midlands.
Midland Red (Express) - Central coach and express services division.
Midland Red (Engineering) - Central engineering workshops at Carlyle Road, Birmingham.

1983

25 December 1983
Midland Red (East) acquired N & S Coaches of Market Harborough. This includes the Market Harborough depot, and coach fleet consisting of seven Fords and one DAF.

1986

1986 First two companies sold
22 December - Midland Red (West).
22 December - Midland Red Coaches - *formally Midland Red (Express)*.

1987

1987 Three more companies sold
5 March - Carlyle Works Limited - *formally Midland Red (Engineering)*.
18 August - Midland Fox - *formally Midland Red (East)*.
10 December - Midland Red (South).

1988

1988 Final company sold
27 January - Midland Red (North).

Chapter One
RESISTANCE TO CHANGE

Midland Red was particularly vociferous in its opposition to the Labour Government's plans for reforming the industry. Back in 1967 the General Manager, J. W. Womar, in his Staff Bulletins, was using words such as 'disastrous' and 'calamitous' in relation to the proposals to set up a Passenger Transport Authority (PTA) in the West Midlands. The PTAs, which would be responsible for public transport in a number of large towns and cities, were originally going to be called Conurbation Transport Authorities (CTA). Walter Womar made it clear that Midland Red did not object to the concept of an Advisory or Co-ordinating CTA (ACTA), which, it felt, could fulfil a really useful function, but it had the strongest objection to the principle of an Operating CTA (OCTA) in the West Midlands because the services outside the proposed area could not provide sufficient revenue to maintain the financial fabric of the company.

The most conspicuous public sign of the company's opposition to nationalisation was the

inclusion of a message on the external side roof panels of some CM6T motorway coaches. These broadcast the company's discontent to a wide audience in Birmingham, Nuneaton, Coventry and London as the coach travelled through the suburbs of the various towns, down the motorway and to the myriad people milling around London's West End and Victoria.

The company's protestations fell on deaf ears, and the inevitable happened on 1 January 1969, ownership of Midland Red being transferred to the National Bus Company. Nothing was to alter overnight, however, and the same buses operated from the same garages with the same management and staff. In fact the transfer of ownership was so low-key that it has proved impossible to establish the exact number or details of vehicles that were taken over by NBC, but with the help of PSV Circle News Sheets your authors have calculated a figure of 1,769. This total included many older BMMO-built vehicles, among them 313 D7s, 110 S14s, 91 S15s, 3 CL2s, 17 CL3s and 64 C5s,

ABOVE It is mid-morning on Sunday 12 November 1967 as CM6T No 5650 unloads its last few passengers at Victoria Coach Station, having departed Digbeth at 08.30. Midland Red was particularly vociferous in its dislike of the Government's nationalisation plans, and these high-speed motorway coaches served as useful mobile billboards, conveying the company's strong feelings on the matter as the vehicles made their regular journeys between the Midlands and London.
Paul Roberts

plus the two D10s —none of them types that are immediately associated with NBC, for none would receive NBC livery.

Little change was seen in the first few years of NBC ownership; indeed it would take almost three years, until the introduction, in 1972, of the white National coach livery and the poppy-red bus livery, for NBC influence to make a serious impact on the public image of Midland Red.

New-vehicle policy evolved at a gentle pace, and 71 BMMO - designed S23s were built and taken into stock under the new regime. However, by 1970 the significant increase in car ownership was not only having an impact on patronage but was also robbing Midland Red of craftsmen for its bus and coach building division, which simply could not compete with the wages being offered by the Midlands-based car manufacturers. The last company-built bus, albeit with a body completed by Plaxton, was S23 No 5991 (UHA 991H), which entered service in June 1970, but as yet there was no NBC corporate identity, and the bus looked exactly the same as those delivered prior to January 1969.

The change from manufacturing vehicles to sourcing them from external suppliers was not without its problems, 52 Leyland Leopard/ Willowbrook single-deck and 33 Daimler Fleetline/ Alexander double-deck buses that had been ordered for delivery in 1970 being significantly delayed. The fact that 'heavyweight' vehicles were unlikely to be available quickly in the numbers required led to an order being placed for 100 lightweight Ford R192s with Plaxton bodywork, the plan being to operate these buses for a period of just seven years. The first 26 of the batch, classified 'S25', were delivered in November 1970.

In the summer of 1970 Midland Red announced that it had ordered 118 Leyland Atlanteans — 68 to be bodied by Alexander and 50 by Metro-Cammell, for delivery in 1971. None of this order, however, reached Midland Red, 60 of the Alexander-bodied vehicles going to Merseyside PTE; the final destination of the other eight was never recorded, so presumably they were never built. Thirty of the Metro-Cammell buses were diverted to London Country Bus Services, whilst the other 20 went to Maidstone & District. History was to repeat itself later in the decade: 20 Park Royal-bodied Atlanteans ordered in 1975 were destined never to join the Midland Red fleet. The following year the order was changed to ECW-bodied Atlanteans, and these were diverted to Ribble. A further instance of vehicles ordered and never delivered involved a batch of 40 Bristol LH/ECW buses that should have joined the fleet in 1975/6 but ended up with Crosville!

As was the case elsewhere, the company had to accept bus types imposed on it by NBC, most notably the Leyland National single-decker, which NBC had developed in conjunction with British Leyland. This new-generation bus was assembled at a purpose-built factory at Lillyhall, near Workington. In 1972 NBC placed an order for 500, so it was inevitable that this type of vehicle would soon find a place in the Midland Red fleet. Indeed, single-deckers — Leyland Leopards, lightweight Fords and Leyland Nationals — would dominate vehicle purchasing throughout the decade, the exceptions being a pair of ECW-bodied Daimler Fleetline CRG6LXs (class D14) ordered by Harper Bros and delivered to Midland Red in 1976 and a solitary 1962 lowbridge ex-PMT Weymann-bodied Leyland Atlantean that was used in Leicester in 1979.

BELOW The anti-nationalisation notice appeared on at least one LC7-class Leopard as well as on the CM6s. Perhaps this was to get the message to a wider audience, because at the time No 5774 was a Leicester (Southgate Street) coach. It was photographed in the old Peterborough bus station on Saturday 19 August 1967 on its way to Cromer, where the message might have caused some bemusement, given that most buses in Norfolk had already been nationalised for nearly 20 years! Peter J. Relf

RIGHT This might not be the image that it would have wished to project, but NBC was nonetheless heir to many older buses, among them 313 Metro-Cammell-bodied D7s. No 4470, which had entered service in February 1956, is seen while on layover in Bearwood bus station on 20 September 1969.
Derek Bailey collection

BELOW The oldest single-deck buses to run for the company during the NBC era were 110 S14s that were built between 1955 and 1959. On Saturday 6 June 1970 No 4672 waits in Railway Drive, Wolverhampton, prior to making its journey to Kidderminster on the 883 via Wombourn and Kinver, which service consisted of just four departures per day.
Derek Bailey collection

The first coaches to be delivered under NBC control were 15 PSU4 Leopards with the new 'Panorama Elite' design of Plaxton coachwork. These 31ft-long 36-seaters were ideal for luxury coach cruises along the narrow roads of Scotland and the West Country. The next batch of 30 coaches was a little more unusual. Designated LC11, these were 36ft-long Leyland Leopard PSU3A chassis, again with Plaxton coachwork, which reverted to the earlier 'Panorama' style but with rather less chrome decoration than normally associated with this style of body.

The other major development that occurred during the early days of NBC ownership was the absorption on 1 January 1971 of the fleet of Stratford-upon-Avon Blue Motors Ltd (better known as 'Stratford Blue'), which had been a wholly owned subsidiary of Midland Red since 1935. The garages at Stratford and Kineton, along with 49 buses and coaches, were placed under the control of BMMO's South Division.

For the first few years under NBC control things outwardly appeared to function just as before, but behind the scenes policies were starting to develop, and the company's resistance to change was doomed to failure. The combined forces of NBC and the West Midlands Passenger Transport Executive slowly but surely changed both the methods of operation and public perception of the company. On 29 March 1974 the inevitable was accepted and, for reasons explained in more detail in the following chapter, the official name of the company became Midland Red Omnibus Co Ltd (MROC).

BELOW There were 17 CL3-class coaches with BMMO chassis dating back to 1954. They originally had Willowbrook bodywork but in 1963/4 were rebodied by Plaxton with a version of its Panorama design, modified to suit the BMMO chassis dimensions. Four members of the class were fitted with a front dome destination box, which helped them show their intended destination when used on long-distance express work. No 4231 was helping out on a London-bound service at Pool Meadow, Coventry, on 25 July 1970.
Derek Bailey collection

LEFT Amongst the oddities taken into NBC stock were the two D10s of 1960/1. On 14 September 1969 No 4943, the 1960-built bus, was photographed at Stafford, where it spent the last seven years of its working life, having been allocated to half a dozen garages in its first three years. Prior to taking a party of Omnibus Society members to Midland Red's Central Works the driver has lifted the side panel, proudly demonstrating the underfloor engine which was the unique feature of the two D10 buses. It came to be expected that BMMO's home-built buses would show imagination and innovation, but this chassis layout would not become commonplace until Volvo Citybuses and Leyland Lions appeared in the 1980s, just as NBC was nearing its end!
Derek Bailey collection

ABOVE During its long history Midland Red occasionally turned to outside manufacturers to supplement its own vehicle-building programme. This increasingly became the case during the 1960s. For its double-deck intake the Daimler Fleetline was the chosen vehicle, the first examples arriving nearly six years before NBC was formed, and by the spring of 1971 a total of 302 had been placed in service. The first 50 were CRG6LX models, designated DD11 by Midland Red, and entered service in 1963; the 149 similar DD12s were delivered over three years, from 1966 to 1968. No 6089 entered service from Wigston garage in July 1967 and when photographed at St Margaret's bus station, Leicester, on 12 October 1969 had recently been repainted, being seen with the new-style fleetname consisting of the full Midland Red name in gold and underlined; it also had smaller fleet numbers. Note that the driver and conductor are still in full Midland Red uniform; it would be a further three years before the corporate NBC uniform was introduced. Derek Bailey collection

FACING PAGE TOP The final Fleetlines ordered by Midland Red were a little different from the earlier examples, having slightly more powerful 6LXB Gardner engines and, more noticeably, dual doorways, facilitating one-man operation. In practice many drivers used only the front doors – something the TGWU backed in the interests of passenger safety; indeed in the Leicester area the centre door would sometimes be taped off using yards of blank Setright ticket roll tied between the stanchions! These DD13s were delivered under the ægis of NBC, 70 buses arriving in the latter part of 1969 and the remaining 33 between November 1970 and January 1971. Pictured barely a month after entering service, No 6187 waits to take up its next duty in Dudley on 27 September 1969. Derek Bailey collection

FACING PAGE BOTTOM The first few examples of the home-built BMMO S23 single-deck buses entered service in December 1968. The S23 was a 36ft-long vehicle, mechanically similar to the S17 type built from 1963 to 1966, having a BMMO 10.5-litre engine and a four-speed semi-automatic gearbox. The main change lay in the body-shell, which was based on that of the CM6 motorway coaches and was thus of six-bay construction rather than seven-bay as hitherto. It had 51 bus seats and was very similar in external appearance to the S21 and S22 dual-purpose classes. Two thirds of the S23 class joined the fleet strength after the NBC era began on 1 January 1969; No 5940 was nearing completion when a party from the Omnibus Society visited the Central Works on 14 September 1969. Sister No 5941 was the final BMMO bus completed at Central Works, the final 50 buses in the batch having their bodywork completed by Plaxton at Scarborough. Maurice Collignon

RIGHT Lightweight buses – Ford R192s with 45-seat Plaxton Derwent bodywork – joined the fleet towards the end of 1970 and certainly looked very different from any vehicles operated hitherto. No 6297 was photographed at Central Works on 18 October 1970 prior to entering service.
Derek Bailey collection

BELOW Surprising acquisitions in April 1970 were five 1960 Leyland Leopard L1s, with 41-seat Weymann Fanfare coachwork, that had been new to the Sheffield 'C' (British Railways-owned) fleet. The coaches were acquired via Amalgamated Passenger Transport at Dewsbury. Converted for one-man operation, they were numbered 6256-60 and entered service in June and July 1970. No 6259 was photographed on 28 November 1970; note the small fleet number above the foremost offside window. All five would be withdrawn in July 1971.
Derek Bailey collection

LEFT The 30 coaches
delivered in 1970 were
designated LC11, being
36ft-long Leyland Leopard
PSU3A models with Plaxton
Panorama coachwork.
These had rather less chrome
decoration than was normally
associated with the style of
body, and indeed the
reversion to the Panorama
seemed a little odd,
considering that the 1969
delivery had comprised
15 Leyland Leopards bodied
with the new Panorama Elite
design. No 6235 was barely
two months old when
photographed on an
excursion to Blackpool on
13 September 1970, despite
having been apparently
put out to grass!
Derek Bailey collection

LEFT Views of Kineton
garage are much less
common than those of
its larger and more easily
accessible counterpart in
the centre of Stratford. This
photograph was taken on a
Sunday afternoon during
December 1970, shortly
before the takeover of
Stratford Blue by Midland
Red. Its vehicle allocation of
12 buses included a greater
percentage of one-man
single-deck buses than
Stratford's, reflecting its
rural location. Several of the
buses seen here were soon
painted into Midland Red
colours, yet just five months
later, in May 1971, two of the
red Tiger Cubs would be
withdrawn. Note that the
name-board over the
entrance bears the full
hyphenated title, whereas
the more common 'Stratford
Blue' name appeared above
the main garage in Stratford.
Paul Roberts

ABOVE Following the takeover of Stratford Blue by Midland Red on 1 January 1971 a rapid repaint programme was put in place. In this view, recorded on 9 June, Stratford bus station plays host to a selection of 73-seat Leyland Titan PD3s. The outer pair have Willowbrook bodywork, the bus on the left being from the first batch of PD3/4s new in 1960, and that on the right one of the final, 1966 batch, on a PD3A/1 chassis; centre-stage is a 1963 PD3/4, bodied by **Northern Counties.** Derek Bailey collection

BELOW Five Leyland Panthers with Marshall Camair dual-door bodies were built for Stratford Blue in 1970 but never turned a wheel in service with the company. This was due to a combination of certification problems and trade-union refusal to accept them, as they were intended to carry 30 standing passengers and had outward-opening centre doors. Inherited by Midland Red in 1971, they were allocated fleet numbers 2031-5, within the series allocated to the

Stratford Blue fleet, and, having been repainted red, were stored in the garage at Adderley Street, Birmingham. This photograph of Nos 31 and 35 was taken on 22 November 1970; on early repaints of Stratford Blue vehicles the original fleet number (without the 2000 added) was reapplied. The Panthers were destined never to run for Midland Red or, indeed, any other NBC subsidiary, eventually passing to Preston Corporation in 1971. Derek Bailey collection

LEFT A number of D7s were repainted during 1971, receiving the latest-style fleetnames and fleet numbers, in yellow, outlined in black. This came as something of a surprise, no D7 having been repainted during the previous 12 months. No 4519 was transferred from Shrewsbury to Leicester (Sandacre Street) in July 1971, being seen awaiting its next duty at St Margaret's bus station in September of that year; note the lack of destination blinds. Despite the repaint it would be withdrawn just three months later, in December.
Geoff Atkins collection

BELOW The new-style fleetnames and fleet numbers – yellow transfers with black edging – represented a great improvement over the previous, plain-gold style. D9 No 4988 makes the point at Leamington garage on 17 September 1972. Note the wide variety of vehicles in the background.
Derek Bailey collection

Chapter Two
THE BLACK HOLE

The 1968 Transport Act was to have far-reaching and devastating consequences for Midland Red, just as General Manager J. W. Womar had predicted. Being part of the National Bus Company meant that, over time, many major policy decisions previously made by the company at top management level would be taken out of its hands. Edicts from NBC headquarters and regional offices were soon controlling events within the company that would set the pattern for the future. Another provision of the Act paved the way for the setting-up of Passenger Transport Authorities in the UK to co-ordinate public transport in some of Britain's largest conurbations. The operating arms of the PTAs were the Passenger Transport Executives (PTEs), and it was the West Midlands PTE, which came into existence on 1 October 1969, that was to have a serious and long-lasting impact on Midland Red's operations.

In a Staff Bulletin dated February 1967 Walter Womar had issued a statement wherein he claimed that the proposed PTA area amounted to just 3% of Midland Red's operating territory but accounted for more than a third of its stage-carriage revenue

and passengers. Furthermore, he claimed, one third of the fleet was operating in the PTA area, which included two-thirds of Midland Red's profitable routes. With hindsight some of his figures could be considered somewhat contentious, but he clearly was keen to stress to staff the seriousness of what was being proposed.

The PTAs were local-authority led, so in the West Midlands the initial task was to co-ordinate operations of the four municipal transport departments of Birmingham, Walsall, West Bromwich and Wolverhampton, which between them had contributed some 2,100 buses. Although these operators had run most of the services within their respective boroughs, several areas of the Black Country which now formed part of the PTA area – notably Dudley, Oldbury, Brierley Hill and Stourbridge – were served almost exclusively by Midland Red. As transport co-ordination was a primary aim of the PTA it was inevitable that these latter would soon come under the watchful eye of the new authority, yet because Midland Red was part of NBC the PTA had no direct powers to control what happened within the company.

ABOVE On 1 January 1974 – four weeks after transfer to West Midlands PTE – No 6023, a Daimler Fleetline CRG6LX with Alexander bodywork (Midland Red class D12), heads for Birmingham's Bull Ring bus station, the vinyl stickers making clear that the bus is no longer owned by Midland Red. This was the only D12 to feature a dual-door layout, having been converted from a standard single-door bus in the company's own central works in an attempt to make it more suitable for one-man operation. No more were altered in this way, although all the D13 Fleetlines were delivered as dual-door buses.
Mike Greenwood

While the future shape of the company was under discussion Midland Red operations continued much as before, although in 1971/2 it closed a number of garages as part of a plan to make its business more efficient. Cradley Heath and Lichfield garages were closed in June 1971, Wolverhampton in November 1971, and Bromsgrove in January 1972. However, on 27 June 1973, following lengthy negotiations, it was announced that agreement had been reached for BMMO's stage-carriage services within the future West Midlands county (to be formed on 1 April 1974, in accordance with the provisions of the Local Government Act 1972) to be transferred to West Midlands PTE, for the sum of £3,600,000. The transfer of ownership took place on 3 December and included 413 vehicles and the six garages at Birmingham (Sheepcote Street), Dudley, Hartshill, Oldbury, Stourbridge and Sutton Coldfield plus the Adderley Street bus park in Birmingham. A total of 1,396 Midland Red staff also moved across to the PTE.

A separate company, Midland Red (Metropolitan) Omnibus Co Ltd, was set up to provide a temporary service conditions structure for the transferred staff. This company then passed to the WMPTE on 3 December 1973 for the nominal sum of £2 in two £1

West Midlands Passenger Transport Executive

FLEET LIST

August, 1975

20p.

shares – one held by the Director General of the PTE, F. J. Lloyd, and the other by Director of Operations James Isaacs (who had transferred from Midland Red). The company was later renamed West

BELOW Four years after the formation of WMPTE enthusiasts in the West Midlands had become used to seeing large numbers of Park Royal- and Metro-Cammell-bodied Daimler Fleetlines in the blue and cream livery, but early sightings of ex-Midland Red Alexander-bodied buses in these colours caused something of a stir. Showing off its immaculate new coat less than two months after changing ownership, D12 No 6072 emerges from Birmingham's Bull Ring bus station on 24 January 1974. Mike Greenwood

1960	Chassis:	Dennis Loline II (Gardner 6LW)		
	Body:	Willowbrook H74F		
		Ex Walsall		

845L 245 HDH

1961	Chassis:	Leyland Atlantean PDR 1/1		
	Body:	Metro-Cammell H76F (OMO)		
		Ex Birmingham		

3231 231 DOC	3234 234 DOC	3237 237 DOC	3239 239 DOC
3232 232 DOC	3235 235 DOC	3238 238 DOC	3240 240 DOC
3233 233 DOC	3236 236 DOC		

1961	Chassis:	Daimler CVG6 (Gardner 6LW)		
	Body:	Metro-Cammell H63R		
		Ex Coventry		

292Y 292 RW	298Y 298 RW	303Y 303 RW	308Y 308 RW
293Y 293 RW	299Y 299 RW	304Y 304 RW	309Y 309 RW
294Y 294 RW	300Y 300 RW	305Y 305 RW	310Y 310 RW
295Y 295 RW	301Y 301 RW	306Y 306 RW	311Y 311 RW
296Y 296 RW	302Y 302 RW	307Y 307 RW	312Y 312 RW
297Y 297 RW			

1961/2/3	'Chassis':	BMMO D9		
	Body:	BMMO H72RD		
		Ex Midland Red		

4945 2945 HA	4968 2968 HA	4987 2987 HA	5023 3023 HA
4947 2947 HA	4978 2978 HA	4995 2995 HA	5036 3036 HA
4949 2949 HA	4981 2981 HA	5014 3014 HA	5044 3044 HA
4953 2953 HA	4982 2982 HA		

1961	Chassis:	Daimler Fleetline CRG6 (Gardner 6LX)		
	Body:	Metro-Cammell H72F		
		Ex Walsall		

| 886L 886 MDH | 888L 888 MDH | 889L 889 MDH | 890L 890 MDH |
| 887L 887 MDH | | | |

8

BELOW On Saturday 23 February 1974 Mike Greenwood visited Dudley bus station to record the gradual metamorphosis from red to blue that was taking place within the local fleet, the changes being reflected in this and the following three photographs. Here D9 No 4945, in its new blue and cream colours, is very much the 'odd man out' as it passes S23 No 5946. Mike Greenwood

Midlands (Metropolitan) Omnibus Co and then, in March 1974, West Midlands Passenger Transport Ltd, being a wholly owned subsidiary of the PTE. This company was wound up in November 1975, when it was absorbed into the main PTE operation.

Following the 1973 takeover Midland Red continued to operate 76 services that ran within the boundaries of the PTE area. Midland Red employees based within this area, at the Midland House headquarters, Carlyle Works and Digbeth, were then issued with special staff passes which permitted them to travel on the routes transferred – but not those operated previously by WMPTE. In addition Midland Red continued to operate its coaching activities and gained cross-boundary services in the Wolverhampton area that had been worked hitherto by WMPTE. In order to provide the capacity required to operate all of the cross-boundary services the depots at Bromsgrove and Cradley Heath were reopened; as a bonus the latter garage also provided space for many of the coaches operated previously from Bearwood, several of the latest C14 motorway coaches being allocated there along with some older vehicles used for other express services originating from Digbeth Coach Station.

ABOVE BMMO S17 No 5563 takes on a good load of passengers for the 10-minute journey to Dudley's Priory Estate. The oval radiator grille that was a hallmark of BMMO-built single-deckers clearly presented WMPTE's coach-painters with something of a quandary when they came to apply the new livery; some buses, like this one, had the entire panel painted blue, whereas many others had simply a blue grille. The difficulty in keeping a mainly cream-coloured bus looking clean is also readily apparent in this view. Mike Greenwood

MIDDLE By mid-1971 Midland Red had placed in service more than 300 Daimler Fleetlines, all of them with Alexander bodywork. No 5277, from the original batch of 50 new in 1963 (as class DD11), was photographed working for its new owner 11 years later, ready to leave Dudley on the indirect but normally busy 120 route to Birmingham. Mike Greenwood

LEFT In the first few months following the transfer it was still possible to photograph all-red clusters of buses. Seen amongst one such group on the vehicle park at Dudley are No 6102, a 1967-built D12-class Daimler Fleetline, and BMMO D9 No 5014, dating from 1962. Mike Greenwood

Of the 413 buses transferred 226 (54%) were double-deckers, of just two basic types. Home-built D9s accounted for 90 transfers, and a mix of 21 D11s, 65 D12s and 50 D13s brought to 136 the number of Daimler Fleetlines which changed hands. Making up the balance were 187 single-deckers, of which 33 were Leyland Nationals, 19 BET-style S18 Leyland Leopards and 135 BMMO types; these last were rather more varied and comprised 14 S16s, 79 S17s, nine S21s, nine S22s and 24 S23s, some of which were less than four years old.

The transfer meant that, on a relatively quiet Sunday, the vehicles involved gained revised legal lettering and (in theory, at least) new 'West Midlands' fleetnames, usually with an accompanying 'WM' logo on the front. These vinyls were printed in gold on a red background designed to match the existing livery, although this was not always the case, especially where the original paintwork had faded.

On Monday 3 December 1973 the buses ran out from their garages bearing their new identity, although it is probable that many a bleary-eyed early-morning commuter did not actually notice the difference. Soon the change became more apparent as buses passed through the paint shops and appeared in the blue and cream colours of WMPTE on routes which had been the haunt of red buses for more than half a century. Almost a quarter of Midland Red's fleet disappeared from the fleet strength overnight, a blow from which the firm would never properly recover. A black hole appeared in Midland Red territory as the heart was transplanted from the company.

TOP S17 No 5695 on layover at Dudley bus station on a sunny afternoon in the spring of 1974, having just completed the 24min journey from Bilston. The bus resembles a patchwork quilt of different reds, both on the front and on the side, where the colour of the fleetname vinyl does not quite match the shade of the paintwork. Fuel and lubricant spills do nothing to help the appearance of the vehicle, and a little 'tender loving care' from the maintenance and cleaning departments would have been beneficial. Paul Roberts

BOTTOM Recently repainted Fleetline No 6287 prepares to leave Oldbury garage one Sunday morning in the spring of 1974. This bus was one of the final batch of D13s delivered to Midland Red in 1970/1 (the class prefix denoting external manufacturers – in this instance 'D' for Daimler – having just been discontinued when they arrived). One of the newest double-deckers involved in the transfer to WMPTE, being just under three years old on change of ownership, it has a new design of front-panel moulding which distinguished this batch from all of Midland Red's earlier Fleetlines. They were built as dual-door vehicles to facilitate one-man operation but between 1975 and 1978, in common with most of the 50 D13s that had been transferred to the PTE, it would be converted to single-door layout. Note that the watering can being used by the driver to top up the radiator is still in Midland Red colours! Paul Roberts

LEFT Nineteen S18 Leyland Leopards, with BET-style bodywork, were involved in the transfer to WMPTE. Some had Weymann bodywork, but most were bodied by Willowbrook, among them No 5232. A lot of care and attention is required to keep a mainly cream livery in a presentable condition, and unfortunately this Stourbridge-based bus was definitely not looking its best when photographed on a winter's day in 1976 in Wolverhampton, in the small bus station (adjacent to Railway Drive) that served out-of-town destinations. Paul Roberts

RIGHT A real mixed bag of buses on display at the former Midland Red Oldbury garage during the autumn of 1974. Coventry Transport had been absorbed by WMPTE with effect from 1 April, and sheltering in the garage is one of its 1958-built Metro-Cammell-bodied Daimler CVG6s, flanked by two D9s and an S17 transferred from Midland Red. The shortage of buses during this period has also brought in a pair of even older Crossley-bodied ex-Birmingham 'Standard' Daimler CVGs dating from 1952 (left), the '87' blind setting revealing that they were used on the busy 'Track', a frequent service linking Dudley, Oldbury and Birmingham. Paul Roberts

LEFT One of 33 Leyland Nationals that passed to WMPTE, is seen leaving Coventry via Upper Well Street en route to Birmingham in March 1974. No 104 is still wearing its smart Midland Red livery, to which new WM vinyls have been neatly applied, but it seems a shame that a modern bus linking two of Britain's major cities is not displaying a destination. The shirt-sleeved driver seems oblivious to the cold, damp weather, so we can reasonably assume that his 15-month-old bus is warm and cosy inside. Tom Moore

Chapter Three
CORPORATE IMAGE RULES

As noted in Chapter 1, in the early years of NBC ownership there was no visible alteration to the existing Midland Red identity on vehicles. The first sign of a change of policy came in mid-March 1972, when repainted vehicles started to be outshopped in a slightly darker shade of red than that used previously. More significantly, in June of that year CM6T No 5652 became the first coach to be painted in the all-white livery of NBC's Central Activities Group; initially this and several C7 coaches thus repainted ran with normal Midland Red coach fleetnames. The dark-red bus livery proved short-lived, being replaced later in the year by an orangey 'poppy' red; the first bus so treated was D9 No 4851, which had hand-painted lettering, with black edging to the fleetname, and very small fleet numbers – regarded by ageing bus spotters with failing eyesight as a significantly retrograde step!

Midland Red continued to use a mix of the pre-1969 BMMO red and the later dark red on repaints but, in September 1972 D13 No 6182 emerged from the paint shop in the full corporate livery of poppy red with white fleetname transfers (without the black edging) and with fleet numbers and legal lettering transfers in grey. The next development came in October 1972, when garages were instructed to paint the wheels of all vehicles grey. The time taken to implement this edict varied considerably, some garages being more enthusiastic than others. Neither 4851 nor 6182 was originally painted with grey wheels. From November 1972 service buses were repainted poppy red, with grey wheels and new-style transfers, although an attractive variation, applied to dual-purpose vehicles, was the 'local coach' livery of poppy red and white. In the first few months, whilst the livery policy was being refined, a number of vehicles received the wrong livery, which had to be rectified subsequently, and, despite the imposition of a supposedly uniform image, older BMMO types continued to be outshopped in pre-NBC red. From February 1974 a

ABOVE CM6T No 5652 would have been chiefly used on the motorway express service to London, so it was evidently enjoying a much easier day when photographed in the coach park at Warwick Castle in June 1972. During the early days of the National white coach livery there were quite a few experiments and variations with regard to the positioning and style of fleetnames and logos. The first Midland Red coach to be so repainted, 5652 retains the pre-corporate style of Midland Red fleetname and fleet numbers and lacks the large **《 NATIONAL** name.
Mike Greenwood collection

ABOVE On Sunday 23 July 1972 C7 No 5786 was employed on an excursion to the East Coast, as is apparent from the sticker in the windscreen. This variation of the livery still features pre-corporate Midland Red fleetname and number transfers but includes a large ⟪**NATIONAL** fleetname, in the NBC approved position, above the rear wheels. As such it provides a marked contrast with a sister C7, still in the company's red and maroon livery.
Derek Bailey collection

6in-deep white band between decks on double-deckers and below the windows on single-deckers was quite an improvement on the rather bland overall poppy red.

The introduction of the corporate livery was the start of a series of changes which ensured that Midland Red would never be the same again. Corporate styles were introduced for many items varying from pocket-size timetables to large notices in bus stations. Next came the introduction of new NBC uniforms for road staff, with the result that, save for a small company name badge, bus and coach crews working for Midland Red were soon indistinguishable from those throughout England and Wales.

The corporate livery policy in respect to coaches meant that only one colour, National white, was allowed. Rapid application of this livery soon made an impact on the public, and hundreds of coaches rapidly became identifiable as being part of the 'National' group. In fact this policy worked so well that, as Paul Roberts (then a coach driver) was to discover, the average member of the public never did quite work out the difference between National Express and National Holidays. By following group policy Midland Red certainly added to the general confusion, because in the early days hitherto dedicated tour coaches, now painted white, were quite likely to appear on an express service the day after they returned from an extended coach cruise. Over the years liveries would be tweaked, but throughout the 1970s the NBC corporate image

swept into most corners of England and Wales. New Leyland Nationals, whether running with Hants & Dorset or Western Welsh, Northern General or Ribble, all looked almost identical to their Midland Red counterparts. Only the fleetname, fleet number and legal lettering gave away the ownership, and this loss of identity resulted in a loss of local pride amongst staff.

During this period the ingress of Leyland Nationals seemed relentless. Full production of the type had commenced at the Workington factory in the summer of 1972, and it was in October of that year Midland Red took delivery of its first example, No 101. This was the only one delivered to the company in traditional livery (albeit the darker shade introduced earlier in the year) and was also significant in initiating a new, three-digit number sequence, following on from Leyland Leopard No 6473, which had joined the fleet a few months previously. The company's vehicles had had four-digit fleet numbers since 1944, so this represented a major change after the best part of 30 years. Every subsequent Leyland National in the fleet arrived in NBC poppy red, so this type more than any other became associated with the corporate image. From 1972 to 1980 ten batches (Midland Red classes N1-N10) were taken into stock, comprising a total of 445 buses. This made Midland Red the second-largest operator of the type within NBC, although not all were on the fleet strength at the same time, 33 vehicles from the first batch having been transferred to WMPTE in December 1973. The vast

ABOVE Pictured at Victoria
Coach Station on 28 October
1972, CM6T No 5658 displays
an experimental style of
fleetname just above the
front wheel arch – small
capitals in grey, heavily
underlined with Midland
Red's house colour.
The transfer had been
applied in July, but already
the red underlining has
started to peel off at the
front. Derek Bailey collection

majority were of the original design, the exceptions
being the final batch of 25, which were National 2s
with 'B-series' fittings; lacking the distinctive roof
pod and fitted with a front-mounted radiator and
larger engine, these looked and sounded very
different from all the earlier Nationals.

The Leyland Nationals purchased by Midland
Red are tabulated below.

The theory was that a Leyland National could
replace a double-deck bus, being licensed to carry
more than 20 standing passengers, which took
potential capacity to 70 – almost the same as that

of a double-decker. This was all well and good until
actual passengers were involved. Although the
passenger capacity of a National was nominally
around 70, real people simply would not wedge
themselves into such a tight space on local routes
and would not stand at the back for fear of being
'trapped' and missing their stop.

The arrival of large numbers of Leyland
Nationals, together with the repaint programme,
ensured that the number of vehicles wearing
corporate livery soon outnumbered those in the
traditional 'Midland' red. However, the application

Leyland Nationals purchased by Midland Red

Delivery dates	Class code	Fleet numbers	Registration numbers	Total
October 1972 – August 1973	N1	101-58	HHA 101-58L	58
August 1973 – June 1974	N2	249-98	NHA 249-98M	50
July 1974 – August 1975	N3	389-438	PHA 489-91M	50
			GOL 392-438N	
October 1975 – May 1976	N4	471-501	JOX 471-501P	31
July – September 1976	N5	502-35	JOX 502-35P	34
August 1976 – May 1977	N6	536-610	NOE 536-610R	75
March 1977 – February 1978	N7	617-664	PUK 617-56R	48
			SOA 657-64S	
April – December 1978	N8	683-724	TOF 683-719S	42
			WOC 720-4T	
February 1979 – January 1980	N9	742-73	XOV 742-60T	32
			BVP 761-73V	
January – September 1980	N10	807-31	BVP 807-22V	25
			EON 823-31V	

445

of the white waistband was never entirely standardised, and an edict issued by NBC headquarters at New Street Square meant that from January 1980 single-deckers would lose this feature upon repaint. The last new bus delivered with a white band was Leyland National 2 No 821, in June 1980.

Whilst the Leyland National was the favoured vehicle for most bus operations two small batches of Ford R1014s, each of 20 vehicles, delivered in 1972 and 1974, joined the 100 R192s that had arrived in 1970/1.

For longer journeys the Leyland Leopard remained a firm favourite, and during the 1970s large numbers were added to the fleet. Until 1974 the bus shell with dual-purpose seats was the norm with 50 Marshall 49-seat DPs (S27 class) arriving in 1973 and a further 50 similar vehicles (S28) in 1974. Incidentally, one of these, No 339 (SHA 639N), was the last vehicle to be delivered with the famous Smethwick 'HA' registration letters, associated with BMMO since the 1920s.

After the DPs came a succession of Leyland Leopard 'grant coaches', which were fitted for one-

BELOW October 1972 saw the introduction of the definitive style of coach fleetname, consisting of 3in-high block letters in poppy red. The solitary C8 Leopard coach, No 5823, received white coach livery in April 1974 and was photographed at Leicester's St Margaret's bus station some six months later, on 5 October. Note that the mouldings on the bodywork required the ≪ NATIONAL to be placed in a non-standard position amidships.
Derek Bailey collection

man operation and equipped with two-leaf power doors. Various batches arrived and looked very attractive in 'local coach' livery of red lower panels and white window surrounds and roof. Plaxton Supreme bodywork adorned this type of vehicle for the next few years, and in each batch there would be a few to full coach specification, delivered in white. In 1976 there were six coaches with 47 seats (type C15) and 21 with grant doors (C16); in 1977 there were six coaches (C17) and 18 grant coaches (C18). The following year saw the arrival of five C19 46-seat coaches, while 1979 brought a dozen 49-seat grant coaches, type C20. In 1980 came 10 Plaxton Supreme IV coaches, classified C21, but these were not quite so generous with legroom, being fitted with 53 seats. (Paul Roberts notes that up to the C14 class of motorway coach, staff always referred to the company class-types but from the C15s onwards this practice ended – probably because the multiplicity of types made it too complicated!) Also in 1980 Midland Red received two further batches of coaches to grant specification, these being the first new vehicles to be given the designation 'CDP'; five with Plaxton Supreme IV bodywork finished in National white, were designated CDP23, while a further 18, with Willowbrook 003 bodywork, in red and white, were designated CDP22. At the same time the 'CDP' code was applied retrospectively to the C16s, C18s and C20s, while classes S27 and S28 similarly became SDP27 and SDP28 respectively.

In 1977 the company added to its stock of Ford buses, the introduction of a new service over restricted roads in Redditch coupled with a requirement for small buses elsewhere prompted the acquisition from London Country of five Transits with Dormobile 16-seat bodies, dating from 1974. The first three filled a gap in the fleet numbers, Nos 441-3, created by the diversion to South Wales Transport of three Leopard coaches intended for Midland Red. When the other pair of Transits was acquired later, the quintet were numbered together as 2121-5.

The three minibuses that were in service at Redditch and Evesham were regularly overloaded, and the company considered that it needed some 25-seat vehicles. With a surplus of seven-year-old Ford/Plaxton buses (not to mention extensive experience of building and rebuilding its own vehicles) it decided in October 1977 to modify No 6391 by removing two bays to establish whether a satisfactory midibus could be produced. The conversion was completed in December 1977, and, reduced in length by 10ft, to 22ft 10in, the bus returned to service at Redditch as a 27-seater, reclassified M2.

The conversion was deemed a success, and two more from the first batch of Fords were similarly converted, re-entering service at Hereford in May 1978. The company announced at this time that it was prepared to undertake up to 40 conversions – 20 F1s (previously designated class S25) and all 20 of the F2 class – and to dispose of these to other NBC fleets if customers could be found; this was in addition to the six that were in the process of conversion for its own use.

Two converted Fords were demonstrated to various NBC subsidiaries, following which City of Oxford Motor Services purchased converted No 6393 in July 1978, and Western National took converted 6359 and 6362 for its Devon General fleet in late 1978. Unfortunately for Midland Red, given the investment it had put in to the conversion programme there were no further NBC orders, save that of a conversion of three Alder Valley ECW-bodied Fords. Midland Red persevered with conversions for its own use in 1978 and 1979, but now with examples of the F3 class, these being reclassified M3. In all, 15 Midland Red Fords (F1s 6359-62/88-93 and F3s 369-73) were converted, although only 14 actually re-entered service as midibuses; the final F3 conversion, No 373, had its body removed and chassis shortened in 1980 but was never completed, the chassis being stored at Carlyle Works for about five years before being scrapped!

LEFT Photographed at Brandon Stadium, six miles to the east of Coventry, in May 1973, S18 Leyland Leopard/Willowbrook No 5237 had been recently repainted in standard NBC livery. The lack of a fleetname on the lower side panels seemed odd in the early days but left space for revenue-generating advertisements, and the 5in-high fleetname, preceded by a 10in 'double-N' logo, on the cove panels made sure that the public would be in no doubt as to the ownership of the vehicle. Note also that NBC-style grey fleet numbers and wheels had now been introduced. Tom Moore

BELOW An early recipient of NBC poppy red was D9 No 5434, here operating a town service in Leamington Spa on a glorious summer's day in August 1973. The driver's nearside cab window is open to improve the flow of fresh air as the bus heads along The Parade, passing the Royal Pump Rooms and Baths. Tom Moore

corporate-identity guidelines issued by NBC in October 1972 stipulated that the wheels of all vehicles be painted grey. BMMO D9 No 5306 had received this refinement by 25 January 1974, when this photograph was taken, despite being still in the old shade of red, with pre-corporate fleetnames and fleet numbers. Seen negotiating a one-way system on its way into Stratford-upon-Avon, it was operating a town service inherited from Stratford Blue and subsequently renumbered.
Mike Greenwood

FACING PAGE BOTTOM When photographed in Tamworth bus station on 23 February 1974 BMMO S22 No 5888 was clearly a prime candidate for repainting. Mike Greenwood

ABOVE Parked in Coventry's Pool Meadow bus station on 27 May 1974, veteran BMMO C1 coach No 3341, dating from 1948, keeps company with 1955-built D7 No 4397. As was the case with many buses converted to driver-trainers, both vehicles have outlived their normal lifespan, but the grey wheels give away the fact that they have entered NBC's corporate era. An unusual feature, albeit normal for the C1 trainers, was the provision of two steering wheels, as well as duplicated foot-pedals. Mike Greenwood

BELOW In October 1972 the so-called NBC 'local coach' livery was introduced to the Midland Red fleet. Thus for a while coaches were once again emerging from the Carlyle Works paint shop in red (albeit white above the waistrail) – but not as long, as a change of policy during this period saw to it that coaches were outshopped in National white. Even the likes of C9 No 5834, here looking every inch a Midland Red vehicle as it passes the National Gallery in London's Trafalgar Square, would not escape this edict and would soon be recalled to Central Works for another repaint, this time in the 'correct' white livery. See page 64. Derek Bailey collection

FACING PAGE ABOVE
In October 1972 No 6418, an S24-class Leyland Leopard/Willowbrook, was painted in an experimental reversed version of the 'local coach' livery; seen at Central Works, it had probably just emerged from the paint shop, judging by its immaculate condition. Shortly afterwards it would suffer extensive accident damage, duly emerging from repair in July 1973 in the standard version of this livery, with red panels below the waist and white above.
Ken Jubb

FACING PAGE BOTTOM
In 1972/3 Midland Red took delivery of 58 Leyland Nationals, of which no fewer than 33 would be transferred to West Midlands PTE on 3 December 1973. Among these latter was No 104, seen at Pool Meadow, Coventry, whilst still with its original owner. The small 'DH' in the destination blind indicates that the bus was allocated to Birmingham Digbeth garage. In 1979 Digbeth would became an all-coach garage, following reorganisation of service routes and buses around Birmingham.
Tom Moore

BELOW Leyland National No 112 leaves Birmingham city centre behind as it heads along New Town Row in the aftermath of a torrential downpour. It is spring 1973, and the bus, just a few months old, is heading towards its home base of Sutton Coldfield. Both the bus and garage would be transferred to WMPTE by the end of the year. Paul Roberts

LEFT Midland Red had long realised the value of good publicity and over the years issued many highly collectable postcards featuring its buses and coaches. If enthusiasts wrote off for a fleet list they might be lucky enough to have a couple of these cards included. The tradition continued into the NBC era, and a set illustrating the new corporate NBC liveries was issued in March 1973. Unsurprisingly, all the vehicles were in ex-works condition, although they weren't necessarily the most modern members of the fleet, as demonstrated by the inclusion of a 10-year-old D9. Although built in 1963 No 5350 was among the first of its type to gain poppy red, complete with new-style fleetnames and fleet numbers and the inevitable grey wheels.

RIGHT Plaxton Panorama I-bodied Leyland Leopard PSU4 (class C9) No 5831 was another relatively old vehicle to be used in a publicity shot, but despite dating from 1966 it looks very smart in its freshly applied 'local coach' livery.

LEFT The BMMO S21s were very much dual-purpose vehicles, witness their comfortable high-backed coach seats, but in this view 1967-built No 5857 has received standard bus livery. The first two S21 repaints were completed in 'local coach' livery but were quickly returned to the paint shop following a change of policy.

RIGHT No 124 was one of the earliest Leyland Nationals to be bought by the company; it was built in 1973 and was thus brand-new when featured on the postcard.

Copyright of the B. & M.M.O. Co. Ltd.

LEFT C12 touring coach No 190 as delivered from coachbuilder Plaxton. New in February 1973, the 12 short (PSU4) Leopards of this second batch were the first coaches to be delivered in National white.

>
>
> ### MIDLAND RED
> Associated with the National Bus Company
>
> FLEET LIST
>
> JANUARY, 1973

N1 101-158	'Chassis': Leyland National 1151/1R/2501; to be built 1972/3
	Body: Leyland National B51F + 22 (OMO)
	Total: 58

101	HHA 101L	116	HHA 116L	131	HHA 131L	145	HHA 145L
102	HHA 102L	117	HHA 117L	132	HHA 132L	146	HHA 146L
103	HHA 103L	118	HHA 118L	133	HHA 133L	147	HHA 147L
104	HHA 104L	119	HHA 119L	134	HHA 134L	148	HHA 148L
105	HHA 105L	120	HHA 120L	135	HHA 135L	149	HHA 149L
106	HHA 106L	121	HHA 121L	136	HHA 136L	150	HHA 150L
107	HHA 107L	122	HHA 122L	137	HHA 137L	151	HHA 151L
108	HHA 108L	123	HHA 123L	138	HHA 138L	152	HHA 152L
109	HHA 109L	124	HHA 124L	139	HHA 139L	153	HHA 153L
110	HHA 110L	125	HHA 125L	140	HHA 140L	154	HHA 154L
111	HHA 111L	126	HHA 126L	141	HHA 141L	155	HHA 155L
112	HHA 112L	127	HHA 127L	142	HHA 142L	156	HHA 156L
113	HHA 113L	128	HHA 128L	143	HHA 143L	157	HHA 157L
114	HHA 114L	129	HHA 129L	144	HHA 144L	158	HHA 158L
115	HHA 115L	130	HHA 130L				

F2 159-178	Chassis: Ford R1014; built 1972
	Body: Plaxton Derwent II B45F (OMO)
	Total: 20

159	HHA 159L	164	HHA 164L	169	HHA 169L	174	HHA 174L
160	HHA 160L	165	HHA 165L	170	HHA 170L	175	HHA 175L
161	HHA 161L	166	HHA 166L	171	HHA 171L	176	HHA 176L
162	HHA 162L	167	HHA 167L	172	HHA 172L	177	HHA 177L
163	HHA 163L	168	HHA 168L	173	HHA 173L	178	HHA 178L

C12 179-190	Chassis: Leyland Leopard PSU4B/4R; to be built 1972/3
	Body: Plaxton Panorama Elite III C40F
	Total: 12

179	HHA 179L	182	HHA 182L	185	HHA 185L	188	HHA 188L
180	HHA 180L	183	HHA 183L	186	HHA 186L	189	HHA 189L
181	HHA 181L	184	HHA 184L	187	HHA 187L	190	HHA 190L

3

LEFT Received in the spring
of 1973, the C13s – Leyland
Leopard PSU3s with Plaxton
Panorama Elite III bodywork
– constituted the first
complete class of coaches
to be delivered in National
white. Nos 191-4 were
48-seaters, whereas
Nos 195-8 were 44-seaters
suitable for extended holiday
tours. Coventry Cathedral
provides a classic backdrop
for No 194, engaged on a
private hire in August 1975.
Tom Moore

BELOW S27 No 221, a 1973
Leyland Leopard/Marshall
49-seater, was allocated
to the ex-Harper Bros garage
at Heath Hayes. These
dual-purpose vehicles were
well suited to the X98
service, which ran from
Hednesford bus station,
where the vehicle is seen
loading, to Birmingham via
the M6 motorway. The highly
visible yellow 'Limited Stop'
blind was appropriate, as the
X98 had very restricted
pick-up and set-down points
at both ends of the route.
Paul Roberts

ABOVE None of the BMMO D7 double-deckers was painted in NBC livery or transferred to WMPTE. The last in service was No 4114, seen in Dudley in February 1973, three months before withdrawal. Keeping it company are S16 No 5138, which would shortly be sent on loan to City of Oxford, and S17 No 5633, destined to be transferred to WMPTE at the end of the year. Maurice Collignon

MIDDLE When the NBC corporate liveries were introduced there was some confusion at Midland Red as to which style should be applied to certain classes of middle-aged coaches and dual-purpose vehicles. Among the vehicles that fell into this category were the S20s, placed in service in 1967, which had Willowbrook bus bodywork fitted with very comfortable coach seats. No 5848 gained poppy-red bus livery in November 1972, but a change of policy saw it repainted in 'local coach' colours just one month later. On 12 January 1975 classmate No 5846, repainted 15 months previously, was photographed taking a well-earned rest in Derby bus station, having completed a journey on the three-times-daily X12 service from Birmingham, scheduled to take 2hr 17min.
Derek Bailey collection

BOTTOM The Ford buses were all allocated to rural garages, so F2 No 178 was quite at home when photographed working a Shrewsbury town service in June 1976. All 20 buses in this batch were delivered in poppy red but also had a white band which followed the trim of the Plaxton Derwent body. No 178, numerically the last, entered service in January 1973. The F2s would have short lives with Midland Red, the entire batch being withdrawn during the autumn of 1979. Bob Jackson

FACING PAGE TOP The C7s were built to full coach specification, with manually operated doors and no PAYE equipment. As such they were repainted in National white until April 1973, following which they were turned out in 'local coach' livery. No 5795 had been so treated in May 1973 and still looks exceptionally smart in this superb shot, showing it travelling at high speed on the M1 near Rugby in August 1974. However, by this time (starting in March 1974) those C7s that had been given 'local coach' colours were being repainted white, No 5795 duly gaining this livery in November!
Tom Moore

FACING PAGE MIDDLE The application of local-coach livery gave the C7s the appearance of still being Midland 'Red' vehicles. No 5815 is seen on Saturday 2 March 1974 parked under the elevated ring road in Coventry's Pool Meadow bus station, with, amongst others, a 1955-built Cheltenham District Bristol KSW for company. Whereas Midland Red resisted the temptation to paint its elderly D7s, the KSW, here operating an enthusiasts' tour, had just received a fresh coat of poppy red, being one of just two such buses to gain the corporate livery when almost 20 years old. Derek Bailey collection

FACING PAGE BOTTOM In January 1974 the final chapter in the paint-shop merry-go-round began, those C9s which had previously been in 'local coach' livery being repainted in National white. No 5828 had received the red and white colours in January 1973 but was repainted just 12 months later, and when photographed on 26 January 1974 in Leicester's Southgate Street coach station it was working an express service to Norwich. In common with eight other C9s it would end up as a cut-down towing vehicle. Mike Greenwood

ABOVE Only one S15 gained poppy red, but it wasn't given fleetnames and did not carry passengers. From May 1973 No 5076 was used as a temporary crew rest room at the new Redditch bus station, having been equipped with tables and 28 seats, and was providing a valuable service to staff when photographed on 31 August. Mike Greenwood

ABOVE The standard Leyland National single-aperture destination box presented a challenge to Midland Red. The company served a vast number of destinations, often with route variations, and for this reason its vehicles traditionally had separate upper 'destination' and lower 'via' blinds. When Leyland Nationals were allocated to a garage for the first time, appropriate new blinds had to be produced that combined the two. Nuneaton-based N2 No 280 was still sadly lacking in this department when parked at its home depot on 27 May 1974, some five months after entering service. Mike Greenwood

BELOW The residents of Fillongley will doubtless already know that this bus is en route from Nuneaton to Coventry, but the lack of a destination display is less than helpful to the general public. N2 No 283 had entered service in Nuneaton in April 1974 but was still waiting for a blind to be fitted when photographed two months later in this small Warwickshire village. Tom Moore

TOP Mike Greenwood paid his only visit to Central Works on 22 March 1974; it was a somewhat grey day, with a mist coming off the adjacent reservoir, but this and the next two photographs give a flavour of the mystique that was still held by Central Works. Being prepared for service was C14 No 305. There were 20 C14s – Leyland Leopard PSU3s with 44-seat Plaxton coachwork – delivered in 1974 as direct replacements for the CM6Ts, and all were toilet-fitted; as such they should really have been CM14Ts! Although they would occasionally venture onto cross-country routes they spent most of their lives on motorway express duties. However, being similar in appearance to many NBC coaches being placed in service all over the country, they never achieved the fame attached to their predecessors. Mike Greenwood

MIDDLE From February 1974 repaints had included a 6in white band applied below the windows on single-deck buses and above the lower-saloon windows on double-deckers, as seen here. Previously allocated to Leamington, D9 No 4859 moved to Wigston garage in July 1973 and thus became familiar sight to Mike Greenwood in his home town of Leicester. Mike Greenwood

BOTTOM Besides offering the joys of freshly painted or brand-new buses and coaches Central Works would often be temporary home to a variety of damaged vehicles; presenting a sad sight, these were usually hidden away around the back, well away from prying eyes. One such was S17 No 5492, a Stourbridge bus which had suffered a devastating fire and would be officially withdrawn in April 1974. It is ironic that this should have been one of the few Midland Red buses to carry the advertisement proclaiming 'We're proud to be part of the National Bus Company – Together we can really go places'; perhaps it should have read '... go to blazes'!
Mike Greenwood

RIGHT Midland Red's operating area included a few tight squeezes, one of the most photogenic being the Northgate arch in Bridgnorth. From the late 1970s buses on the 890 route from Wolverhampton also worked a local town service, to Sydney Cottage Estate, which took them through this arch, and the new arrangement put an end to double-deck working, for obvious reasons! Emphasising the point in September 1980 is 1974-built N2 Leyland National No 290, which had begun life without a white band but had this applied at a later repaint. Bob Jackson

BELOW On Bank Holiday Monday 27 May 1974 seats on day tours were still at a premium, so much so that service buses had to be drafted in to cope with the demand. Excursions from Birmingham normally loaded in the city's Bull Ring bus station (rather than in Digbeth Coach Station, as might have been expected), although these three are seen in Edgbaston Street, just by the exit; presumably there was no room inside to accommodate them. Contrasting with Nuneaton's S23 No 5933, Tamworth-based F3 Fords Nos 369 and 370 were just a month old at the time. Mike Greenwood

LEFT The Harvey Walk footbridge provides a splendid view of buses in Leicester's St Nicholas Circle. Here, in June 1974 – shortly after the introduction of white waistbands – smartly presented D9 No 4916 makes its way into Leicester from Wigston, where it was allocated. It is rare to see a Midland Red bus displaying a single-digit route number, the 8 being a Leicester local service; prior to 1973 it had been numbered L8.
Mike Greenwood

BELOW The front-end design of many of Midland Red's single-deckers did not allow for the white waistband to be continued right around the vehicle. On 15 June 1974 S17 No 5448 was parked at Leicester St Margaret's bus station, where a faulty flap-catch has left exposed the normally hidden filler for the front-mounted radiator. Note, on the hoarding in the background, the Inter-City advertisement whereby British Rail, with its faster journey time to London, is seeking to entice passengers away from National Express!
Mike Greenwood

RIGHT In the spring of 1974 Stafford-based S17 No 5504 became one of the first BMMO-built buses in the area to gain the newly introduced white waistband. As such it presented a welcome change from the previous all-red livery, so when it unexpectedly appeared in Cannock bus station the photographer temporarily forsook the comfort of his Harper Bros ECW-bodied Daimler Fleetline to take this shot. Paul Roberts

RIGHT Tamworth garage's No 5193 was originally fitted with 48 high-backed seats and had a black roof, but by the time it was photographed leaving Lichfield bus station during the summer of 1974 it had been converted to a 53-seat bus. It was also one of the first S18s to be adorned with a white waistband. There were no collieries in the city of Lichfield, but contract services were operated locally from several coal mines in Staffordshire and Warwickshire. The double-deck bus just visible in the distance is an ex-East Kent Guy Arab IV belonging to H&M Coaches of Chasetown. Paul Roberts

RIGHT Remember the BMMO S22 at Tamworth seen earlier in the chapter and in urgent need of a repaint in February 1974? Well, here is the same bus following a visit to the paint shop and consequently looking very much smarter. By now allocated to Swadlincote garage, it would have been a regular visitor to Burton-on-Trent's Wetmore Park bus station, where it is seen on 1 June 1975. The destination uses the simplified form of 'Ashby' because squeezing the full name 'Ashby-de-la-Zouch' into the aperture provided would be something of a challenge! Derek Bailey collection

LEFT S26 Leyland Leopard No 6461 clearly displays its intended journey as it heads out of Coventry along Corporation Street in June 1974. The driver appears to be making light work of the heavy steering as he starts to swing his bus into Upper Well Street. There were 13 vehicles in this bus-seated class; a further 152 broadly similar Leopards, designated S24, S27 and S28, had coach seats and were painted in the 'local coach' livery of red and white. The S24s had Willowbrook bodywork; the others were all bodied by Marshall. Tom Moore

BELOW Freshly repainted from 'local coach' colours, S20 No 5842 shows off yet another livery variation for the class at St Margaret's bus station in Leicester on 10 July 1976. From mid-June a new style of 'double-N' logo in red and blue, as used on coaches, had been applied to buses, the poppy-red base colour requiring this to be on a white square; at the same time side fleet numbers were discontinued save for those near the fuel filler cap. This new livery application had been trialled in April on D13 No 6181 and newly delivered N4 Leyland National No 492, the latter also receiving a white waistband, but a further year would elapse before this feature was applied as standard to new Nationals. Derek Bailey collection

ABOVE From 1 October 1974, when the DVLC's computer at Swansea came into operation, vehicle registrations were issued by new Local Vehicle Licensing Offices. Midland Red's head office fell within the area covered by Birmingham LVLO, which had taken over registration letters used previously by local motor-taxation offices within the new West Midlands county, and this broke the company's 52-year association with the 'HA' registration letters issued by the Smethwick (and latterly Warley) local motor-taxation office. The last bus with an 'HA' registration was S28 Leyland Leopard/Marshall No 339 (SHA 639N), which was also one of the few new vehicles to enter Midland Red service at Heath Hayes garage; it later moved to Wellington, where it is seen in this view. The first 20 vehicles of this batch, Nos 319-38, were registered PHA 319-38M. Trevor Follows

RIGHT The 10 S28s that followed on from No 339 were registered GJW 40-9N, and initially it seemed a little odd that new Midland Red vehicles should be registered with marks more commonly associated with the former municipalities of Birmingham, Walsall and, as in this case, Wolverhampton. Regardless of this, passengers boarding No 348 in Pool Meadow bus station, Coventry, in September 1977 could expect a comfortable, coach-seated ride, even if it was a relatively short journey. Tom Moore

LEFT Patriotic Union Flags are in evidence to celebrate the Queen's Silver Jubilee in June 1977 as N3 Leyland National No 413 makes its way through Rugby on a town service, the heavy rain having put such a shine on the road that it is almost possible to inspect the underside of the bus. At the time of this photograph it was just over two years old but still had no white relief other than on the front bumper. Tom Moore

BELOW In the days of municipal transport in Walsall the 865 route had been operated jointly by Midland Red and Walsall Corporation (whose buses showed '65') and had linked Dudley with Stafford via Walsall – a journey of almost two hours. Eventually, after Walsall Corporation Transport had been absorbed by WMPTE, Midland Red ceased to operate the Walsall–Dudley section but had the Cannock–Stafford portion to itself. This much-curtailed route no longer required double-deck buses, and in July 1976 another all-red Leyland National, N4 No 480, was photographed leaving Walsall's Bradford Place bus station for Stafford. The continuing decline in passenger numbers would dictate that by 1984 the service, by now renumbered X65, consisted of just one round-trip, on Tuesdays and Fridays only! Tom Moore

LEFT Two Leyland Nationals challenge readers to 'spot the difference' while operating on Rugby town services in June 1977. Just three months old at the time of the photograph, N7 No 622 displays the latest embellishments of a white waistband and a new-style 'double-N' logo on the front; N3 No 410, at work since March 1975 and bearing the British Leyland roundel, lacks any form of relief other than the front bumper. Tom Moore

BELOW Seen passing Kenilworth's historic clock, C15 Leyland Leopard/Plaxton Supreme No 447 had only recently entered service when photographed in July 1976 and, aside from a 3in-high 'MIDLAND RED' fleetname in red above the front wheel arch, was indistinguishable from other such coaches entering service throughout NBC territory. These 47-seaters were regular performers on both excursions and National Express work. Tom Moore

ABOVE The practice of splitting batches of Leyland Leopards into full coach and 'grant coach' specification began in 1976. C16 No 451 continued the JOX-P registration series begun with the C15s but was fitted for stage-carriage work. It too was delivered early in 1976, with white 'double-N' logos, just before the new style was introduced, being seen here at Weston-super-Mare in 1980. Paul Roberts

LEFT Even the Silver Jubilee had an NBC corporate livery application. Midland Red painted two D12s – Nos 6044 and 6054 – in silver and blue, and Central Works also painted three Bristol VRs (one for Eastern Counties, two for Hants & Dorset) in a similar scheme. It was fitting that No 6044 should have been used to carry visitors to the Royal Show at Stoneleigh in July 1977, although the driver's casual striped shirt was probably not the image that Midland Red or NBC would have wished to project. Tom Moore

FACING PAGE TOP Perhaps this is the view that British Leyland should have used to sell the Leyland National to the Americans! An idyllic scene in August 1978 features N7 No 664 carrying tourists to and from Anne Hathaway's Cottage, right opposite the bus stop. This popular attraction on the Shakespeare Trail is just over one mile to the west of Stratford-upon-Avon in the village of Shottery, which until 1971 had been served by Stratford Blue. Tom Moore

FACING PAGE BOTTOM Unusual acquisitions from PMT in 1979 were five lowbridge Weymann-bodied Leyland Atlanteans (one dating from 1959, one from 1960 and three from 1962) plus two highbridge Northern Counties-bodied Daimler Fleetlines of 1963 vintage. The only bus to enter service was a 1962 Atlantean, which was numbered 2910 and allocated to Leicester, being seen here in the city's St Margaret's bus station on 14 April 1979. Derek Bailey collection

ABOVE In 1979 D12 No 6007 was treated to a special livery in celebration of Midland Red's 75th anniversary. It is pictured at Stoneleigh, working a shuttle service to the Royal Showground from Coventry, in July of that year. Tom Moore

ABOVE Late in 1979 two Ford Transits with Dormobile bodies were reallocated to Leicester's Sandacre Street garage, where, from 8 December, they were used mainly on services that gave some cover for Post Bus operations that had been discontinued in the Billesdon and Market Harborough areas. M1 No 2125 is seen heading into Leicester along Humberstone Road during its brief period of operation; the pair would be withdrawn in May 1980. Note the petrol prices per gallon at the BP petrol station. Mike Greenwood

BELOW During the period 1977-9 no fewer than 15 Ford R-series buses were shortened to become midibuses, reducing their seating capacity from 45 to 27. They were not particularly successful in rebuilt form, and most had been withdrawn by the time of the six-way split of Midland Red in September 1981. No 370, pictured working for Midland Red (West) in May 1982, was one of the exceptions and after withdrawal in 1990 went on to be preserved by the Birmingham & Midland Motor Omnibus Trust at The Transport Museum, Wythall. Trevor Follows

TOP Summer Saturday express services from the Midlands to coastal resorts were still very much in demand in June 1983, when CDP20 Leyland Leopard/Plaxton No 739 was photographed unloading in Paignton bus station. The value of grant coaches lay in the fact that they were just as suitable for these long journeys as their white-painted sisters yet could operate stage-carriage routes at other times. Another Midland Red coach, probably the main 'service car' on the 958 route, can be seen angle-parked on the left of the picture. Geoff Atkins collection

ABOVE An edict from NBC headquarters meant that from January 1980 single-deck buses would lose their white waistband upon repaint. The last new bus to be delivered with this feature, in June, was N10 Leyland National 2 No 821, pictured in Loughborough bus station in May 1981. Only 10 further N10s had been delivered without the white band, these being the last new vehicles to enter service with Midland Red Omnibus Co, and the company split in September 1981 would effectively signal an end to the fleet's uniform identity. Geoff Atkins collection

Chapter Four
AN INDEPENDENT INTERLUDE

Like most large bus companies, Midland Red had from time to time taken over other operators within its territory, yet in the 1950s and '60s its operating area had been relatively stable. Regulation of services and operators by the system of Traffic Commissioners had prevented any sudden or significant changes, other than by acquisition, and the public could rely on familiar operators providing services running to timetables that were long established. Any alteration to times or fares had to be presented to the local office of the traffic commissioner and, if considered contentious, subjected to a public inquiries in the traffic courts. Objections could come from other operators already serving a particular area, and sometimes British Railways would object too. Services tended to be very settled, and operators made little or no alteration to timetables that had been tried and tested, often over decades. Any company would find it very difficult to expand its field of stage-carriage operations, should it wish to do so.

One way that Midland Red could expand was by the acquisition of private operators. Many such companies had been founded by young men returning home after World War 1, and these same people began to reach retirement age in the 1950s, '60s and '70s. In an industry that was now struggling with falling patronage and reducing profits or even now suffering trading losses the appeal to later generations of taking over the family business was diminished, and this meant that some well-established firms were open to offers.

The sizeable Leicestershire operators Kemp & Shaw, Boyer's and Brown's Blue were acquired between 1955 and 1963, but there were no more takeovers in the latter half of the 1960s. However, this situation changed dramatically in the 1970s. Midland Red had the prospect of a large cash injection as a result of selling its operations in the West Midlands, and this enabled it to go on a spending spree. Several more companies sold out in the early part of the 1970s, and the purchase of

ABOVE The business of G. Cooper & Sons of Oakengates was acquired on 15 October 1973. The newest vehicle was this Bedford YRT with a 53-seat Plaxton Elite Express body, bought in January 1974. It was retained for a short period but never repainted, although when photographed at Wellington garage on 17 August it had been fitted with a Midland Red destination blind and had a small white fleet number (2148). It also had a '900' route-number label in the windscreen, suggesting a return to its old stamping-ground between Wellington and Oakengates.
Derek Bailey collection

these long-established firms was one way that the company planned to rebuild its strength. The operators acquired were based in Shropshire and Staffordshire, the first being G. Cooper & Sons of Oakengates, in October 1973, soon followed by the Green Bus Co Ltd of Rugeley, in November 1973. In 1974 T. Hoggins & Sons of Wrockwardine Wood and Harper Bros (Heath Hayes) Ltd, incorporating Tudor Rose Coaches of Sutton Coldfield, were acquired. These four companies had between them operated 120 vehicles, of which 99 went onto Midland Red's books, although only 66 were used.

During this round of takeovers Harpers was the only company to provide additional premises as well as buses and coaches. Heath Hayes garage was home to a mixture of Midland Red and ex-Harper vehicles from 1974 until a brand-new facility opened at Cannock on 4 February 1977. There was a wonderful period for enthusiasts when former Harpers ex-London Transport RTLs, with full Midland Red legal lettering, could be seen on all-day front-line service while the acquired newer Titans and Fleetlines were being repainted in the recently introduced poppy-red livery. During Midland Red's two-and-a-half years operating from Heath Hayes garage the local bus fleet benefited from the use of six Leyland Titans (three PD2s and three PD3s), eight Daimler Fleetlines (four CRG6LX and two CRL6, plus a further two CRG6LX delivered new and classified D14 by the company) and one lightweight Bedford SB5 bus. Also added were 26 coaches, these comprising 14 Leyland Leopards, six Bedford VAMs and six Bedford SB5s. When the fleet and staff moved to Cannock the services of all the conductors were dispensed with, and the Leyland Titans withdrawn.

A smaller addition towards the end of the decade involved the remnants of National Travel (Midlands) Ltd. This short-lived company had been formed in December 1973 with the revival and renaming of the dormant South Midland Motor Services Ltd. Early in 1974 it took over Birmingham-based Worthington Motor Tours Ltd and Don Everall Travel Ltd of Wolverhampton, which well-known names were retained for just two years in National Travel ownership. In 1977 the Midlands operation was absorbed by National Travel (West) Ltd, but things were not to remain stable for long. On 9 December 1978 the garage in Hurst Street, Birmingham, closed, that at Bilston, near Wolverhampton, following suit at the end of the month. This meant that from January 1979 National Travel (West) had no operational garages in the West Midlands Traffic Area, and a result 12 modern coaches passed to Midland Red, although eight of these were merely on loan. Ten were Bedford YMTs, with Plaxton Supreme coachwork, whilst the other two were Willowbrook Spacecar-bodied Leyland Leopards, fitted out as team coaches for the West Bromwich Albion and Wolverhampton Wanderers football clubs.

Meanwhile, on 1 April 1978, Midland Red had taken over the Telford-area services operated hitherto by the remaining members of the Shropshire Omnibus Association co-operative. No vehicles were involved.

Finally, mention should be made of Monty Moreton Ltd, which since the 1920s had provided stage-carriage services, works contracts and excursions in the Nuneaton area. When the company ceased trading in April 1980 a couple of its bus routes were taken over by Midland Red, but again no vehicles were acquired by Midland Red.

BELOW With its acquisition on 7 September 1974 of Harper Bros (Heath Hayes) Ltd Midland Red gained a further 16 Bedfords. These did not include any examples of the YRQ model, but the Duple Viceroy-bodied pair acquired from Coopers eventually appeared at Heath Hayes, each having suffered engine failure. It was rumoured that they were to be withdrawn, the pair having been unceremoniously 'dumped' at the back of the patch, but eventually Midland Red obtained the non-standard engines required, and they returned to service, both now painted in dual-purpose livery and converted for one-man operation. Paul Roberts

ABOVE Following their return to service the two ex-Cooper YRQs were used mainly on local stage-carriage routes and contract services. At this time it was not uncommon to employ vehicles that had high steps, and the pair were often used to operate the same duties as the service-bus Fords. However, on Saturday 7 May 1977 No 2147 demonstrated its versatility, taking a day off from bus work to transport West Bromwich Albion football supporters to the match at Leicester, being seen here in Western Boulevard, close to the Filbert Street ground. It would be a happy journey home, West Brom beating Leicester City 5-0! Derek Bailey collection

BELOW The yard at Worcester's Padmore Street garage was used as a storage area for vehicles in transit. A visitor on 27 May 1974 was No 2154, a Seddon Pennine IV which had joined the fleet upon the takeover of Green Bus Co of Rugeley, acquired by Midland Red on 5 November 1973. It was fitted with a Midland Red destination layout and repainted in poppy red before re-entering service at Tamworth garage, but it had extremely heavy steering; in less than a week the union put a ban on the bus, and it never ran for Midland Red again, although not officially withdrawn until September. Also visible in this shot are another stored ex-Green Bus Seddon – Plaxton-bodied coach No 2149 (WDG 379J) – and a pair of withdrawn BMMO CM6 coaches. Tom Moore

ABOVE At first glance this bus looks like all the other 140 Midland Red Fords, but the Shropshire registration betrays the fact that it had been acquired with the fleet of T. Hoggins & Son of Wrockwardine Wood, taken over on 6 January 1974. XUX 417K was allocated fleet number No 2181 and, after a period in store, moved to Heath Hayes garage, where it is seen parked on Tuesday 16 March 1975. Its duty that day was to operate a football special service to Wolverhampton Wanderers' Molineux stadium.
Derek Bailey collection

LEFT With effect from 7 September 1974 Midland Red took over the operations of Harper Bros, of Heath Hayes, and the routes were renumbered into the Midland Red series. It was impossible to show these three-figure route numbers in the destination display of ex-Harper vehicles, so large metal route-number plates were used. This ex-St Helens RT-type AEC Regent III, No 9, became Midland Red No 2209 but only on paper; 22xx-series transfers were not applied to older buses in the fleet. It is seen shortly after the takeover, having paused for a photographic stop in Lichfield Road, Leacroft, while running light from Heath Hayes to Cannock. Paul Roberts

ABOVE During the winter of 1974/5 ex-Harper coaches were despatched at regular intervals to Central Works to be painted in National white. Some passengers thought that the coaches actually went faster when they reappeared in their smart new livery! Here two Duple-bodied Bedford SB5s dating from 1971, Nos 2258 and 2272, offer a 'before and after' comparison in the vehicle park at the back of Heath Hayes garage. All 26 coaches would be repainted by the summer of 1975, within a year of the takeover. Paul Roberts

BELOW At Heath Hayes garage there was much speculation as to the likely fate of non-standard lightweight bus No 2247, which was always known to staff as the 'bread van'. This 1972 Willowbrook-bodied Bedford SB5 disappeared into store for a period, but rumours of its demise were quashed when it returned to the garage in the summer of 1975, freshly painted in the latest livery of poppy red with a white band. No 2247 had been the last SB5 delivered to Harper Bros; the Duple Bella Vega coach pictured alongside, No 2270, built in 1969, was the oldest of the six ex-Harper coach-bodied SB5s taken into Midland Red stock. Paul Roberts

ABOVE In Midland Red parlance a driver's stand-by shift was always referred to as being 'on show-up'. One such turn on a miserable Sunday in the autumn of 1976 allowed the photographer the chance to rearrange these four Daimler Fleetlines into order, by age. Nos 2229, 2232 and 2234 and D14 No 439 represent one from each pair delivered to Heath Hayes in 1970, 1971, 1973 and 1976. The left-hand pair, with Northern Counties bodywork, have had their destination apertures enlarged to accommodate Midland Red blinds; of the two on the right, bodied by ECW, No 2234 still has an original Harper Bros blind, while the D14 has a standard Leyland National display. Paul Roberts

BELOW Six Harper Bros Leyland Titans – three PD2s and three PD3s – were taken over by Midland Red and painted in corporate livery. Three of them, in a seemingly random selection, had their destination screens altered to the Midland Red standard, while three were left with a single screen. Freshly repainted PD2A/27 No 2228, seen parked at Heath Hayes in the spring of 1975, has received the full conversion and displays a smart new advertisement that leads us neatly into our next chapter! Paul Roberts

Chapter Five
YOUR WHITE COACH AWAITS

Midland Red had been associated with coaching and long-distance express work since the 1920s. It had established itself as one of the premier coach-tour operators in the UK and, along with several other BET companies, notably Southdown and Sheffield United Tours, was recognised as providing a top-class product. In 1967 almost 19,000 passengers enjoyed such a holiday with Midland Red. Until this time touring holidays were operated by senior drivers with a wealth of experience and accompanied by a 'conductor' – the equivalent of a modern-day courier. Coaches employed on these duties offered luxurious travel with seating capacities that would soon come to be regarded as uneconomically low; by necessity the vehicles were of smaller size, partly because of regulations and also because of the narrow roads encountered in Scotland and Devon and Cornwall, areas which were particularly popular with the company's customers, and the desire to allow passengers extra space and generous legroom kept capacity as

low as 30 or even 26. For a while following absorption by NBC these holidays continued to be operated with very little alteration: seating capacities crept up to 36, then 40, but essentially coaches built to Midland Red's seat-layout specification could still be seen on Coach Cruises in the early 1970s.

Things began to change in 1972, when NBC's Central Activities Group was formed to bring holidays and express services under central control. This period also saw the start of mass marketing and the concept of 'economies of scale' – something NBC saw itself as being well placed to develop. In round figures NBC subsidiaries operated 3,000 coaches out of a total fleet strength of 21,000, so this aspect of the group's operations, accounting as it did for about 14% of the fleet, had considerable potential for development. The biggest change came with the introduction of the corporate coach livery of all-over white with a large '≪ NATIONAL' on the side

ABOVE The first Midland Red coaches to receive National white were the CM6 and C7 classes, repainting commencing in June 1972. However, CM6T No 5674 was one of the last members of its class to be so treated, in September 1973, being seen here at London's Victoria Coach Station on 21 October. *Derek Bailey collection*

and small company 'identifier' name over the front wheel arch. Inevitably, given that about 20 NBC subsidiaries operated holiday tours, there were overlaps in both pick-ups and destinations, and the Central Activities Group also sought to remove these anomalies and to rationalise certain aspects of their operation.

Besides the detrimental effects of cheap foreign package holidays and an increasing personal mobility created by the spread of car ownership, a problem particularly associated with early days of the 'National white' era was that customer loyalty, often built over decades by high-quality coach operators, was all but lost. Whilst the ever-growing fleet of white coaches no doubt impressed senior management at NBC headquarters it was often a nightmare for passengers trying to find their coach at large interchanges such as Victoria or Cheltenham.

BELOW An early repaint in white, in July 1972, C7 No 5800 was photographed in August 1975 heading south along the A5 (Watling Street) through Towcester on the daily stopping service from Birmingham to London. Whereas C14s travelling on the parallel M1 were scheduled to complete the trip in 2hr 15min, this once-a-day run left Birmingham at 08.35 and was due to arrive in Victoria at the very precise time of 13.21 – a journey of 4hr 46min; it did, however, serve 26 towns and villages en route. Tom Moore

LEFT In the 1970s holiday tours were usually operated from Easter to autumn, following which Midland Red would delicense a portion of its coach fleet, storing the vehicles throughout the winter. This made it easy to fit them into an off-season repaint programme, and the white coach livery soon became a familiar sight; between October 1972 and April 1973 Midland Red put 72 coaches through the paint shop, these comprising seven CM6s, 16 C7s, 15 C10s, 19 C11s and 15 C12s. Initially there were no additional markings to identify National Holidays or National Express coaches, so vehicles could be easily be used for either duty. In this August 1975 view C12 No 6449 is setting off from Coventry on a holiday tour, which will also help promote the National image in Scotland. Tom Moore

BELOW C11 No 6234 was one of the class to be given an early repaint into 'local coach' colours and then quickly upgraded, donning National white in February 1973. Although nominally still enjoying full coach status, it was being employed stage-carriage work when photographed passing though the village Stoneleigh on 6 July 1978 on the shuttle service between Coventry and the Royal Show. Tom Moore

LEFT Leyland Leopard PSU3 No 2036 had been new to Stratford Blue in May 1970, just seven months before its parent company was taken over by Midland Red. In April 1971 it was painted in all-over BET red, and just over two years later, in June 1973, it received full National white coach livery. Its Alexander Y-type bodywork nevertheless ensured that it always stood out amongst the other Leopards in the fleet, and in July 1975 it was photographed speeding along the M1 in Northamptonshire, bound for its then home of Digbeth Coach Station. Tom Moore

RIGHT No 2269 was one of four Leyland Leopards with Duple (Northern) Commander III bodywork which had been part of the Harper Bros fleet and dated from 1968. The coach is seen heading through Birmingham's Bull Ring, close to Digbeth Coach Station, in June 1976. Tom Moore

BELOW By the summer of 1975 numerous coaches from various NBC subsidiaries had been painted in National white, and although enthusiasts could still recognise vehicles as belonging to different companies the sea of white became a source of confusion for ordinary passengers. This was particularly so when coaches gathered en masse at interchange points, as here at London's Victoria Coach Station, where an inspector looks to be practising Irish dancing as he alights from ex-Harper Leyland Leopard No 2255! This vehicle is standing at the front of Bay 3, ready to act as a relief coach on the 501 Motorway Express to Birmingham.

RIGHT On 7 July 1976 Paul Roberts, working a one-week holiday tour to Devon, was asked by an inspector at Torquay's Torwood Street coach station if his coach could be used on a trip when not otherwise required, and this led to the unusual sight of a Midland Red coach and driver operating a local excursion from Torquay to Totnes and Dartington Hall 'on hire to Greenslades Tours'. Seen awaiting its passengers' return from their afternoon tea break, No 2256, a short 45-seat Leyland Leopard/Duple, had originally been licensed to Tudor Rose Coaches of Sutton Coldfield, a subsidiary of Harper Bros. Paul Roberts

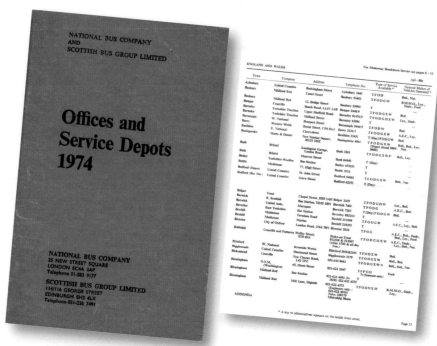

LEFT From the driver's point of view there were many advantages to being part of a national set-up. In due course all coach drivers were issued with a directory, 'Offices and Service Depots', which listed phone numbers and addresses for every NBC and Scottish Bus Group depot, as well as many workshops and bus stations. In the days before mobile phones just having access to a telephone that didn't need feeding with money could be a major asset during a crisis, and it was very reassuring to know that back-up – ranging from a roadside mechanic to a replacement vehicle – was always available not too far away.

BELOW Reciprocal arrangements between all NBC and SBG subsidiaries made life a lot easier for tour drivers. Here C9 No 5834 gets a 'wash and brush-up' courtesy of the Eastern Scottish depot at Galashiels whilst on a Scottish Borders tour in the summer of 1975. This vehicle had been restored to full coach status when repainted from 'local coach' livery in February 1974. Paul Roberts

LEFT From December 1973 no fewer than 18 C7s were repainted from 'local coach' colours into National white coach livery, No 5811, seen in Worcester, having been upgraded thus in May 1974. The final example so treated was No 5795, in November 1974, following which, with the exception of acquired vehicles, all of Midland Red's coaches were in white livery.
Mike Greenwood

LEFT The C9-class Leopards were withdrawn in November and December 1976, and between March 1978 and October 1980 eight of the 15 coaches were converted to towing vehicles. Here, in Coventry in April 1979, one has come to the aid of C17 Leopard No 614, which had been operating the lengthy cross-country 577 service from Cannock to Brighton via Oxford, Aldershot and Chichester. By an interesting coincidence No 614 was destined also to end its career as a towing vehicle. Tom Moore

RIGHT Late in 1978 Midland Red took delivery of its last front-line tour coaches, equipped with reclining seats with armrests. Nos 725-9, designated C19, were Plaxton-bodied Leyland Leopard PSU3Es seating just 46 in an 11m coach, which gave the passengers extra legroom. Attempts were made to restrict the vehicles to tours and private hires, but they occasionally strayed onto much more punishing National Express work, and the effect on the once pristine interior trim soon began to show. No 726 was, however, being used as intended when photographed on a 'Private Charter' at Coventry Cathedral. Tom Moore

LEFT July 1981 witnessed the arrival of the last new vehicle delivered to Midland Red Omnibus Co Ltd. Fitted with a 51-seat Plaxton Supreme IV GT body, No 832 designated C25 was very much a one-off. A 12m Leyland Tiger TRCTL11/3R, with a 218hp TL11 engine (which wasn't much more powerful than the 185hp 680 unit fitted to the company's Leyland Leopards), it also broke new ground in being the only fully automatic coach in the fleet at the time. In the event it remained unused by MROC, passing to Midland Red (Express) at the split and finally entering service in mid-September 1981. It was photographed in Nottingham Victoria bus station in March 1982. Geoff Atkins collection

Chapter Six
MAP AND LOCAL IDENTITIES TAKE HOLD

In common with a number of other NBC subsidiaries Midland Red had interpreted the early corporate-livery instructions somewhat loosely, initially omitting the white waistband. Eventually, however, it had to toe the line, and the adoption of this feature (from 1974) had a particularly pleasing effect on 'home-built' BMMO buses such as the S17s and D9s, which hitherto had been seen only in a single unrelieved colour.

The service networks had drifted along in a format that had barely changed over many years, despite falling patronage. NBC's real task lay in making them more cost-effective and responsive to changing demands. The first town within Midland Red territory to be subjected to a major network revision was Redditch. This had become a designated New Town in 1966, being intended as an overspill for Birmingham, and rapid expansion in the early 1970s resulted in the construction new bus-only roads, as well as changing travel patterns. From 13 March 1976 a batch of 15 Leyland Nationals started running in

the town, bearing a large stylised 'Reddibus' logo in orange and green between the axles at skirt-panel level, which represented a radical departure from traditional and, indeed, corporate fleetname styles.

Car ownership was on the increase everywhere, and costs were rising, creating inflationary pressures; alterations would have to be made in order to produce financial savings, hopefully with minimal effect on patronage. A little later in 1976 the Viable Network Project was launched, the name reflecting precisely what was required in the future. As the first survey of its kind it was jointly conducted with NBC Consultancy Services and independent consultant Colin Buchanan & Partners. Many sources were used, including waybill and revenue figures, loading censuses and comments from passengers and staff. Midland Red was the first company within the NBC to instigate such a radical scheme, and, as a pilot, it started as a small regional experiment rather than a project covering the whole of its operating area.

ABOVE 'Reddibus' was the first local identity to be introduced by Midland Red, on 13 March 1976; from this date Redditch benefited from an enhanced network, initially with six new and nine older Leyland Nationals. Posed for an official photograph when new, N4 No 488 shows the 'Reddibus' name, which was applied in orange and green. Four more new Nationals would be added in the spring of 1977.
Mike Greenwood collection

By 1977 the results of the VNP survey had been analysed, and changes were being implemented in Stratford-upon-Avon, Evesham and Kidderminster. This resulted in the first widespread deviation from the corporate livery: in addition to the 'double-N' and Midland Red fleetname a local identity name was displayed on all buses, but on single-deckers this was applied on an additional white band which appeared above the windows. The imaginative titles were 'Avonbus' (Stratford-upon-Avon), 'Wayfarer' (Evesham) and 'Wendaway' (Kidderminster). Such additions would scarcely be regarded as ground-breaking in the 21st century, when buses are frequently adorned with a multitude of vinyls, but in an era dominated by drab, single-colour liveries it was perceived as an adventurous development in product branding. VNP was a successful exercise inasmuch as it gave bus operators and local authorities more reliable figures from which to calculate subsidies and grants. NBC saw it as the way forward, and it was introduced nationwide. In October 1977 VNP became MAP – Market Analysis Project – but this worked on very similar concepts to VNP. Paul Roberts was working as a driver at Midland Red's brand-new Cannock garage at this time and has memories of large numbers of surveyors assembling in the canteen at anti-social hours. The 05.00 starts and 01.00 finishes were part and parcel of daily work for busmen but must have come as a shock to the mainly youthful MAP surveyors! So comprehensive was the study that by the end of the project every scheduled departure on every route and contract had been surveyed. Each passenger on a bus under survey was quizzed as to his or her journey patterns, not just a random sample, the aim being to get the most comprehensive possible picture of bus usage.

When the survey for a particular area had been completed the results would be analysed and a new route network implemented. In a couple of cases more drastic action meant garage closures. The first occurred when the 'Hunter' scheme was introduced in Nuneaton on 12 May 1979, resulting in the closure of Hinckley garage. The second was the closure of Kineton garage in Warwickshire, which had been acquired by Midland Red had with the takeover of Stratford Blue on 1 January 1971; closure came as a result of the Leamington & Warwick MAP scheme, introduced on 31 May 1980.

By the late summer of 1981 more than a dozen local brand-names had been introduced, and these are listed opposite, along with the areas affected.

After extensive research involving other enthusiasts, as well as discussions with Midland Red management staff in office at the time, your authors have concluded that there was never a formal MAP analysis undertaken in Leicester. The Leicester-area operations were, however, heavily scrutinised, and it seems likely that MAP techniques were employed in designing a new network that was introduced on 31 May 1980. This was necessitated by a 20% reduction in subsidy from Leicestershire County Council, one consequence being the closure of Sandacre Street garage. Another was the redeployment of the company's last conductors, the city having until recently been the last bastion of the rear-entrance D9 double-decker, which formally bowed out on 31 December 1979.

VNP and MAP Schemes

Trial Scheme

13 March 1976	'Reddibus'	Redditch

Viable Network Project

28 May 1977	'Avonbus'	Stratford-upon-Avon
23 July 1977	'Wayfarer'	Evesham
5 November 1977	'Wendaway'	Kidderminster

Market Analysis Project

11 March 1978	'Wandaward'	Hereford
1 April 1978	'Tellus'	Telford
13 January 1979	'Severnlink'	Worcester and Bromsgrove
7 February 1979	'Lancer'	Coalville and Swadlincote
12 May 1979	'Hunter'	Nuneaton (Hinckley garage closed)
1 September 1979	'Mercian'	Tamworth and Lichfield
31 May 1980	'Chaserider'	Cannock and Stafford
31 May 1980	'Leamington & Warwick'	Leamington (Kineton garage closed)
24 November 1980	'Hotspur'	Shrewsbury and Ludlow
5 April 1981	'Rugby – Midland Red'	Rugby
11 July 1981	'Ridercross'	Banbury

ABOVE As a result of the Viable Network Project services in Stratford-upon-Avon were recast with effect from 28 May 1977, the 'Avonbus' name being introduced on timetables, bus stops and vehicles operating in the area. The branding does not sit particularly comfortably in the only space available on this Alexander-bodied Daimler Fleetline, D13 No 6271, pictured operating a town service in Stratford in January 1978. Tom Moore

RIGHT When a new VNP or MAP network was introduced to an area it would often be accompanied by an intake of new vehicles. Such was the case in Kidderminster, where new N5 Leyland Nationals launched the 'Wendaway' scheme on 5 November 1977. These were Phase 2 Nationals, which incorporated several modifications: the batteries were repositioned at the front of the bus to improve weight distribution, the seats had a slightly different rake, and there was a new finish to some interior fittings, the grab-rails, luggage pen and decency panel at mid-vehicle step position being now black, in lieu of the previous brightwork. Coasting down Comberton Hill, Kidderminster, No 533 heads into town centre on its way from the railway station on 24 April 1984. Dick White

ABOVE Single-deck buses provided a useful space above the windows for a broad white stripe (assuming it remained attached to the bus – which, as can be seen, was not always the case) and a new MAP name. Tellus was an ancient Roman goddess, and ever since the name was used to market buses in the Telford area, from 1 April 1978, debate has continued as to why it was chosen! Buses were based at Wellington garage, where, on 29 May 1978, BMMO S21 No 5864 was outnumbered by a bevy of Fords.
Derek Bailey collection

LEFT Introduced on 7 February 1979, 'Lancer' was the name used for the network of services around Coalville and Swadlincote. Some of its routes served Burton-on-Trent, where S24 Leyland Leopard/Willowbrook No 6427 was photographed travelling along High Street on 21 April 1979. A one-time dual-purpose vehicle, by now in bus livery yet retaining its coach seating, it is missing the NBC 'double-N' on the upper white band. Two and a half years later the 'Lancer' name would be abandoned by the newly formed Midland Red (East) company.
Mike Greenwood

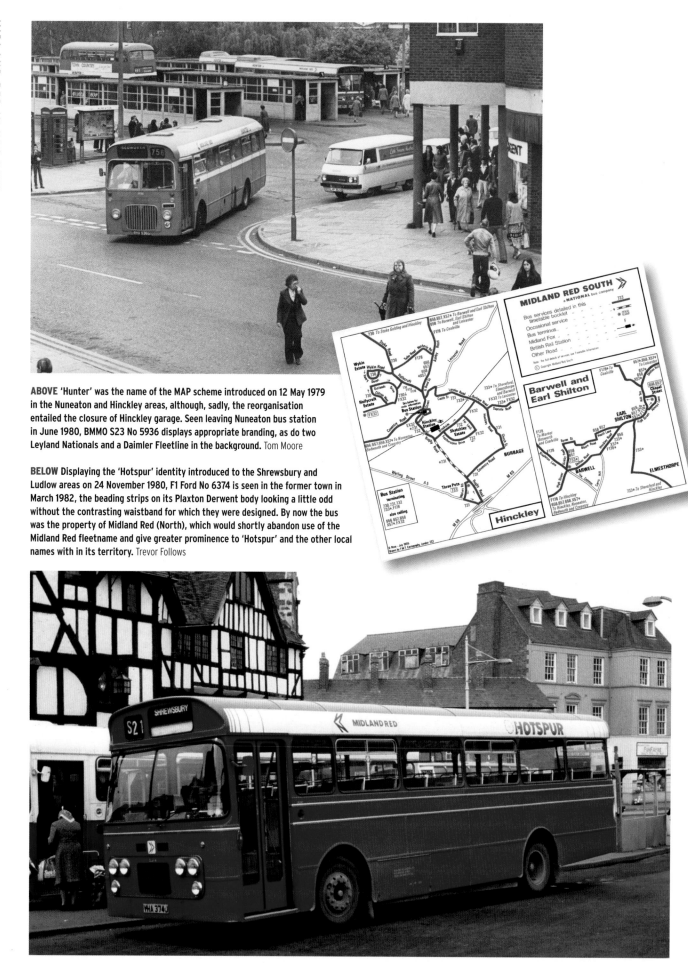

ABOVE 'Hunter' was the name of the MAP scheme introduced on 12 May 1979 in the Nuneaton and Hinckley areas, although, sadly, the reorganisation entailed the closure of Hinckley garage. Seen leaving Nuneaton bus station in June 1980, BMMO S23 No 5936 displays appropriate branding, as do two Leyland Nationals and a Daimler Fleetline in the background. Tom Moore

BELOW Displaying the 'Hotspur' identity introduced to the Shrewsbury and Ludlow areas on 24 November 1980, F1 Ford No 6374 is seen in the former town in March 1982, the beading strips on its Plaxton Derwent body looking a little odd without the contrasting waistband for which they were designed. By now the bus was the property of Midland Red (North), which would shortly abandon use of the Midland Red fleetname and give greater prominence to 'Hotspur' and the other local names with in its territory. Trevor Follows

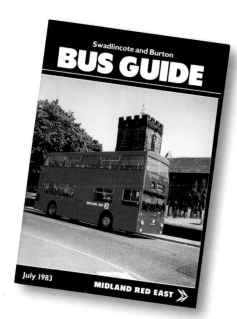

Swadlincote and Burton
BUS GUIDE

July 1983   **MIDLAND RED EAST** »

RIGHT Midland Red buses in the city of Leicester displayed no branding but gained enthusiasts' attention for a different reason: until the end of 1979 some local services remained in the hands of the company's last surviving half-cab double-deckers. The photographer was up well before dawn to capture this scene, complete with a Mother's Pride making its early-morning delivery. With just 10 days to go before withdrawal, 1964-built BMMO D9 No 5370 loads in Charles Street on 22 December. Conductors would last a little longer, their last working day being 31 May 1980. Mike Greenwood

BELOW Although in the early 1980s large swathes of its territory were being subjected to major changes as a result of MAP schemes, these were not the only events affecting Midland Red. Saturday 28 February 1981 was a particularly significant day in the history of the company inasmuch as it witnessed the last BMMO-built buses running in normal service. S23s Nos 5953 and 5977 worked their last trips in Nuneaton and Leamington, while here the photographer has captured the last pair to run in Rugby. Having just returned to the garage, No 5930 is studied by a somewhat disconsolate group standing alongside sister No 5937. Trevor Follows

Chapter Seven
THE SIX WAY SPLIT

Some of the Market Analysis Project cuts had been drastic, but it soon became apparent that they had not been enough on their own to keep the company afloat in the long term.

Extensive economies in staff and vehicles had to be made to achieve a satisfactory financial return in 1980, but for 1981/2 the anticipated shortfall was nevertheless expected to be around £5 million. With financial support of only £2.3 million something obviously had to be done, and customary management action on its own seemed not to provide a solution for the company's long-term financial stability.

In February 1981 the decision was taken to close the Head Office (Midland House), Divisional offices and Central Works and to divide the company's operations into four regional bus companies and one coach company, each county council only receiving the level of service provision for which it was prepared to pay. The proposal was put to staff, who objected most strongly, some going so far as

to predict that smaller operating companies would not be viable. However, on 31 March 1981 a trade-union delegation met with NBC representatives, and the proposal to divide the company was accepted in principle. At a subsequent board meeting it was decided that a sixth company, a much-reduced Midland Red Omnibus Co Ltd, should look after the engineering side and serve as a property-holding company.

No secretarial department was included in any of the new companies' organisations, as some statistical, financial and legal work would be carried out by neighbouring NBC subsidiaries. In consequence large numbers of administrative and head-office staff were declared redundant, their roles generally passing to the supporting companies.

The division of Midland Red Omnibus Co into smaller units did not result in the dire consequences that some had forecast; indeed it was deemed a great success, to the extent that was used as a model by other NBC subsidiaries in the South of

ABOVE On 1 January 1983 the entire Midland Red (Express) fleet was renumbered in the 5xx series. Soon afterwards four of the C11-class Leyland Leopards, which had had their Plaxton bodies removed at Carlyle Works, re-entered service with new 49-seat ECW coach bodies fitted to the refurbished chassis. This was done for financial reasons, as, according to one engineering manager at Digbeth, the four rebodied coaches cost approximately the same price as three brand-new ones. However, they were soon discovered to suffer badly from noise and vibration, comparing poorly with brand-new Leyland Tigers, and as a result they were swiftly relegated to less prestigious work. No 549, based on the chassis of C11 No 6249, is seen parked at Bristol in May 1983, shortly after entering service; just visible beneath the front bumper is the retractable step that was fitted to these vehicles in an attempt to make access easier in the days before 'kneeling' suspension. *Trevor Follows*

England as they sought to relate their activities more closely to local needs and to match their costs to their income.

The new Midland Red companies commenced operation on 6 September 1981 (the four bus companies being based on the previous four administrative divisions) and were as follows:

Midland Red (North) Ltd, covering the former North West Division and operating 230 vehicles from six garages (Cannock, Ludlow, Shrewsbury, Stafford, Tamworth and Wellington), with secretarial support from the Potteries Motor Traction Co.

Midland Red (South) Ltd, covering the former South East Division and operating 163 vehicles from five garages (Banbury, Leamington, Nuneaton, Rugby and Stratford), with secretarial support from the United Counties Omnibus Co.

Midland Red (East) Ltd, covering the former North East Division and operating 181 vehicles from four garages (Coalville, Leicester, Swadlincote and Wigston), with secretarial support from the Trent Motor Traction Co.

Midland Red (West) Ltd, covering the former South West Division and operating 183 vehicles from six garages (Bromsgrove, Evesham, Hereford, Kidderminster, Redditch and Worcester), with secretarial support from the Bristol Omnibus Co.

Midland Red (Express) Ltd, operating 82 coaches from one garage (Digbeth), with secretarial support from the Bristol Omnibus Co.

The Bristol company also provided support for the Midland Red Omnibus Co (Carlyle Works).

During the early months of their existence there was frequent vehicle transfers as the new companies sought to lick their businesses into shape. Each developed a different marketing strategy in respect of the use of the Midland Red name, and there was a similarly mixed enthusiasm for retaining the MAP-inspired area names.

Midland Red (North) chose to phase out the Midland Red name altogether from April 1982 as vehicles were repainted; in its place the local identity names – 'Chaserider', 'Hotspur', 'Mercian' and 'Tellus' – assumed a stronger presence, effectively becoming the fleetnames (and continuing as such until privatisation of the company). Minibuses were purchased in large numbers from 1985, the first examples entering service at Stafford in May and at Shrewsbury in November; in 1986 further minibus networks were introduced, in Lichfield (April),

Telford (May) and Cannock (June), while later that year (in August) services in Tamworth were also revised using minibuses.

At Midland Red (South) the first significant change came in May 1982, when repainted vehicles began to emerge with 'Midland Red South' fleetnames applied in standard NBC style. From around this time the MAP names started to disappear, the 'Rugby' local identity in April and 'Leamington & Warwick' in May 1982; 'Avonbus', 'Hunter' and 'Ridercross' survived a little longer, eventually being phased out from March 1983. Minibuses were introduced in October 1986 in Banbury, Rugby, Leamington, Nuneaton and Stratford-upon-Avon, those at the last-mentioned being painted in a new-style Stratford Blue livery.

Midland Red (East) arguably made the most dynamic and far-reaching changes to its identity. The 'Lancer' MAP name soon fell into disuse, and early in 1982 the company became the first within NBC to make a departure from the corporate image by introducing a new livery of unrelieved dark red, albeit initially retaining the NBC-style Midland Red fleetname. However, livery experiments continued, and it took until May 1983

Midland Red West Travel Guide image courtesy of the Omnibus Society Library

ABOVE The delivery of Leyland Tiger No 832 was not quite the end of the vehicular story as far as MROC was concerned, the company having previously ordered 12 Leyland Leopards, but, with the split looming, the chassis were placed in store unbodied. Subsequently they were allocated to Midland Red (Express), which, with the age profile of its fleet rising beyond an acceptable level, had them fitted with Willowbrook 003 bodies and thus gained a dozen new vehicles suitable for express work. Following on from the Tiger as Nos 833-44, they entered service in June and July 1982. Most of the vehicles in this October view at the National Exhibition Centre were being used as car-park shuttles in connection with that year's Commercial Motor Show, among them a MAN and a Leyland-DAB articulated bus, which, after initial service in Sheffield with South Yorkshire PTE, were on loan to Midland Red (Express) from their respective manufacturers. Tom Moore

to arrive at the definitive scheme. Applied to a recently acquired ex-London Transport Fleetline, this was dramatically different from anything seen previously: the front third of the bus was yellow and the remainder dark red, the split being diagonal. From mid-September this livery became standard for new and repainted vehicles. At first a small 'Midland Red' fleetname was retained, being applied to the company's first new ECW-bodied Olympians, but a change of name had long been rumoured, and the game was somewhat given away when the late-1983 edition of the Yellow Pages guide for the Leicester area used the name 'Midland Fox' alongside a list of East's existing addresses and telephone numbers; the guide also referred to its offices as 'lairs'! The official announcement came shortly afterwards, and on 15 January 1984 Midland Red (East) was formally re-titled, the new name soon appearing on vehicles, accompanied by a stylised elongated fox.

Livery and name changes aside, developments at the Leicester-based company included the acquisition in December 1983 of the long-established business of N&S Coaches, of Market Harborough, including the Market Harborough depot as well as seven Fords and one DAF, all with Plaxton coachwork. In 1985 new Ford Transit minibuses, branded 'Fox Cub', were introduced to Coalville, Hinckley and Leicester, and by March 1986 the minibus fleet numbered 177 such vehicles.

Midland Red (West) initially retained the corporate livery and Midland Red fleetname, together with the MAP-inspired local identities, although 'Severnlink', 'Wandaward', 'Wayfarer' and 'Wendaway' were gradually phased out from July 1984, 'Reddibus' following suit from April 1986. In its early days, however, the new company was preoccupied with events in the Hereford area, which, under the provisions of the Transport Act 1980, had since 27 July 1981 been used by the Government to assess the effects of deregulating local bus services. As a result Midland Red (West) suffered intense competition from local

independents, and to combat this the company in April 1983 took over the Hereford city routes worked hitherto by G. H. Yeomans, together with the long-standing Yeomans route between Hereford and Credenhill, the deal including the acquisition of two of Yeoman's Bedford YMTs with Duple coachwork. Later in the year, as part of a rationalisation programme, Bromsgrove garage was identified as being surplus to requirements, closing its doors for a second and final time in September.

From 1985 Midland Red (West)'s excursions and private hires were marketed under the 'MidWest' name, using coaches being painted in an attractive livery of white, maroon and gold. The introduction, with effect from 23 November, of 59 Mercedes-Benz minibuses in Worcester brought with it a further new livery of yellow with a blue skirt and rear, the two colours being separated by an orange band; these vehicles bore the fleetname 'Citibus' together with the city's coat of arms. Further minibus services were introduced in the Kidderminster area on 8 March 1986 using the 'Wyre Forest Shuttle' brand name and in Redditch on 19 April 1986 as 'Reddilink'. July of that year witnessed the introduction of an attractive new livery for full-size buses – cream and red with a black skirt, the 'Midland Red West' fleetname, applied to the cream area, being in red with black shading. Services in the West Midlands were won by tender from 26 October 1986, and the company operated these from Digbeth using Leyland Nationals.

The headquarters of Midland Red (Express) was at Digbeth, Birmingham, this being the company's only garage. Its 82 coaches comprised 74 Plaxton-bodied Leyland Leopards dating from 1970 (C11s) to 1980 (C21s), plus seven Duple-bodied Leopards acquired from Harper Bros and one Plaxton-bodied Tiger (C25).

In 1984 NBC's coaching subsidiaries were reorganised whereby each was linked to a neighbouring bus company, and in the case of Midland Red (Express) this was Midland Red (North). In early May 1985 the company was re-

LEFT A regular intake of new Leyland Tiger and second-hand Leopard and Tiger coaches kept the average age of the Midland Red (Express) fleet at a low level, but a more unusual addition, in June 1983, was a solitary Roe Doyen-bodied Leyland Royal Tiger – only the second of its type to enter service anywhere. No 555 was photographed on 22 January 1985 in Barford Street alongside Birmingham Wholesale Market, behind Digbeth coach station; home-based coaches were parked here in order to free space inside the coach station for the busy National Express interchanges, which saw mass departures every two hours. Mike Greenwood

titled Midland Red Coaches Ltd, a change of name aimed at getting away from its image of being an 'express-only' operator.

Digbeth ceased to be an operational garage from 1 February 1986, following which the Midland Red Coaches fleet was based at the MROC premises at Carlyle Works. With the move to Carlyle Works the link with Bristol Management Services was severed, because secretarial and accountancy support was performed locally. Also in 1986 Midland Red Coaches gained a large number of school contracts from Allenways in Birmingham. Several drivers transferred, but the additional operations were covered by the existing fleet. However, as already noted, at deregulation Midland Red (West) gained a substantial number of contracts in the West Midlands and reopened Digbeth as an operational garage to run these. It therefore made sense to transfer the Midland Red Coaches fleet back to Digbeth, and on 26 October 1986 the business and vehicles were placed under the control of Midland Red (West).

The renaming of Midland Red (Express), to which reference is made above, had a further benefit inasmuch as it helped overcome confusion with Midland Express. Launched on 28 March 1983, following a meeting attended by the managers of the four bus-operating companies, this was a marketing and operating concept, the original plan being to introduce a common livery for limited-stop services serving Birmingham; at this time such services still terminated at the city's Bull Ring bus station, so connections from one route to another were very easy for the passenger. The livery followed the 'venetian blind' pattern recently introduced by NBC for its subsidiaries' coach liveries, the colours being in this case red and yellow; the **_MIDLAND EXPRESS_** name, in an italicised, non-corporate style, appeared on vehicle sides, an abbreviated **_ME_** similarly on the front. Most of the services thus branded were numbered in the 'X' series, and quite a few headed out of Birmingham using the area's expanding motorway network; the

X66, for example, travelled along the A38M Aston Expressway and then turned south along the M6 before heading east along the M69 to the outskirts of Leicester, thereby offering running times comparable with train travel. The original Midland Express concept soon changed, however, and before long the name was being used to market services such as the X60 (Telford-Derby-Nottingham) and X67 (Loughborough-Leicester-Coventry), neither of which ventured anywhere near Birmingham.

As explained earlier, the Midland Red Omnibus Co Ltd survived the split, albeit in much-reduced form and now trading as Carlyle Works. No longer an operating company, it had to redefine itself, providing

X68	LEICESTER — COALVILLE — ASHBY — NORRIS HILL — SWADLINCOTE — BURTON (Limited Stop)
X69	LEICESTER — COALVILLE — SWANNINGTON — ASHBY — SWADLINCOTE — BURTON (Limited Stop)
167	LEICESTER — COALVILLE — RAVENSTONE — ASHBY
169	LEICESTER — COALVILLE — SWANNINGTON — ASHBY — NORRIS HILL — SWADLINCOTE — BURTON

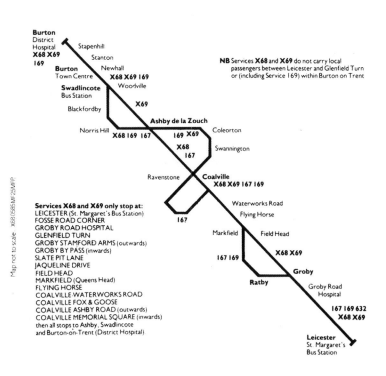

Map not to scale X68 0585 MF25MFP

engineering services on the open market, although in practice in the early days the paint shops and vast workshops found that a lot of business still came their way from the four new Midland Red operating companies. NBC had informed the management that Carlyle Works would have to be viable by the end of 1982. Accordingly the company started to find and develop other business, including a major painting contract to repaint the erstwhile ATV van fleet in the colours of the new franchise-holder, Central Television. Some of the local independent bus and coach operators, who were in competition with the Midland Red operating companies, also turned to Carlyle for assistance. However, by far the most significant development came in 1984, when the company completed the first of what would eventually number hundreds of 16-seat minibus conversions, based mainly on Ford Transit vans. These little buses would be very much in demand as privatisation loomed, Devon General being one of the earliest and keenest customers. A few were built on Freight Rover Sherpa chassis, but the Transit remained the firm favourite, and at times the works would contain several dozen of these little workhorses in various states of conversion and wearing an array of different colours and new-style liveries.

By the mid-1980s, notwithstanding its efforts to streamline its operations, NBC had been overtaken by events beyond its control. April 1983 had seen the Conservative Government (in office since 1979) re-elected with an increased majority, and, given its desire to reduce the size of the public sector, this effectively sealed NBC's fate. The beginning of the end came with the Transport Act 1985, which among other things stipulated that NBC should be privatised. The Act received Royal Assent in October,

and in the 12 months before the privatisation process began in earnest the operating areas of certain NBC subsidiaries were adjusted ready for the grand sale, as the Government wanted companies to be sold off in more manageable packages. Such adjustments were not required with Midland Red, which had, of course, already gone through the process in 1981. It is often stated that the company was broken up in readiness for privatisation, but this was not the case; as explained earlier, the division had become necessary in order to try to resolve major financial issues even after the MAP schemes had been implemented. Big was no longer beautiful, and smaller, self-contained companies with a slimmer infrastructure were seen as the profitable way forward.

Following deregulation on 26 October 1986 the companies faced new challenges, as open competition was now the name of the game. For managers there was also the prospect of new and risky ventures ahead as NBC looked to sell off its 72 constituent companies. The first company sale was actually completed prior to deregulation when National Holidays was sold on 14 July 1986. Midland Red (West), by now incorporating Midland Red Coaches, became the 10th company to be sold by NBC, when, on 23 December, it was purchased by its management. The next sale of a Midland Red company was that of Carlyle Works, to Frontsource on 5 March 1987. The same year saw two other companies sold – Midland Fox to a management buy-out jointly with Stevenson's of Uttoxeter on 19 August, and Midland Red (South) to Western Travel on 10 December. Finally, on 27 January 1988, Midland Red (North) was sold to Drawlane. Midland Red's NBC days were over.

BELOW Traditionally Midland Red had not participated in coach rallies, but following the split Geoffrey Clarkson, General Manager of the newly formed Midland Red (Express), entered vehicles in the well-known events at Blackpool and Brighton as a way of raising the profile of his company. Here Paul Roberts is a picture of concentration as he manœuvres Plaxton-bodied Leyland Tiger No 556 through the driving test at the 1984 British Coach Rally at Brighton. Interestingly registrations commencing 'A55' were withheld by the DVLC to avoid the possibility of this seemingly innocent combination being manipulated to represent something offensive; accordingly Nos 556-8 were registered A656-8 VDA.
Dick White

MIDLAND RED (EXPRESS) – MIDLAND RED COACHES

LEFT Midland Red (Express) fleet livery was initially corporate NBC white, with National Express or National Holidays names as appropriate. However, a pair of Mercedes-Benz minicoaches delivered in the spring of 1984 received a red and black scheme that rekindled memories of traditional Midland Red coach livery, this being another innovation by the company's new manager as part of an attempt to restore local pride. No 570 is seen departing the Sandwell Transport Festival in May of that year. Trevor Follows

RIGHT Ten Leyland Leopards, Nos 774-83, delivered early in 1980, were the highest-capacity single-deck coaches ever delivered to Midland Red, having 53 tightly packed non-reclining seats. In February 1985 Midland Red (Express) continued its 'traditional livery' theme, three of these previously white Plaxton-bodied coaches receiving a livery consisting of a black roof and window surrounds, a deep white band below the windows and red lower panels. These vehicles bore 'Midland Red Coaches' fleetnames in a style similar to that applied the minicoaches, and in May 1985 the company name was formally changed from Midland Red (Express) Ltd to Midland Red Coaches Ltd. On a glorious late-summer day in 1985 No 574 (formerly 774) was photographed at Crawley bus station while engaged on a private charter. Stuart Turner

RIGHT Midland Red (Express) Leyland Leopard 843 was withdrawn in October 1982 following a serious accident in which the coach overturned and its Willowbrook body was damaged beyond repair. The chassis was eventually rebuilt and fitted with a 218hp Leyland TL11 engine and a new 44-seat (plus toilet) Plaxton Paramount coach body; renumbered 553 and re-registered Q553 UOC, it returned to service in July 1984. Later it was downseated to 42 to make room for a small servery, rendering it suitable for National Express 'Rapide' work, it received appropriate livery in June 1985 and was photographed at Victoria Coach Station in London in September of that year, having arrived from Birmingham. Trevor Follows

ABOVE Many National Express services travelled along motorways for long distances, and during the early 1980s some were upgraded to 'Rapide' status. These newly branded services had a host or hostess serving drinks and snacks and normally provided an on-board toilet; new technology also meant that videos could be shown, although this facility was not necessarily appreciated by occasional travellers, many of whom preferred to watch the countryside go by rather than view a film in a darkened coach. Midland Red (Express) needed more high-specification vehicles to operate these routes, prompting some second-hand purchases; by now, however, NBC's traditional tie to Leyland vehicles was fast fading away and new types were introduced. A 49-seat Bova Europa integral, No 505 had been new to North Devon in 1984 and was acquired in April 1985, being seen here a month later at Victoria Coach Station, shortly after its new owner's renaming as Midland Red Coaches. Trevor Follows

RIGHT Arguably the most unlikely vehicles to join the Midland Red Coaches fleet were five Alexander-bodied Daimler Fleetlines that had been new in 1971 to W. Alexander & Sons (Fife) and were acquired in June 1986 from dealer Martin's of Middlewich. These were used on two bus services – Solihull-Balsall Common and Coventry-Balsall Common-Solihull – that had been operated previously by Heart of England Tours and later by West Midlands PTE. Midland Red Coaches operated these routes on a short-term PTE contract, and No 59 is seen at Pool Meadow bus station, Coventry, early in October 1986; halfway through that same month the Fleetlines would be replaced by five Leyland Nationals borrowed from Midland Red (West). At deregulation, on 26 October, none of the tendered services was secured by Midland Red Coaches, and thus ended the company's incursion into local-bus operation. Trevor Follows

RIGHT In 1986 seven MCW Metroliners, seating 55 passengers upstairs and just 17 downstairs, were delivered for use on the expanding 'Rapide' network, the first three arriving in January, the remaining four in May. Here the driver and hostess of No 502 check for traffic as they depart Victoria Coach Station for Birmingham in April 1986. Trevor Follows

MIDLAND RED (NORTH)

ABOVE In August 1981 Midland Red Omnibus Co purchased from Trent four Alexander-bodied Daimler Fleetlines, and a start was made on converting them for one-man operation. However, by the time the work had been completed the company's operations had been divided, and whilst three of the buses were allocated to Midland Red (West) No 2543 went to Midland Red (North), being seen here in Ludlow in April 1982. Trevor Follows

LEFT Midland Red (North) chose to abandon the old Midland Red fleetname, giving greater prominence to the MAP-inspired local-identity names, which now appeared on a colour band unique to each area. The company's first new buses were a batch of 10 ECW-bodied Leyland Olympians delivered in 1983; in July of that year, when just two months old and still gleaming, No 1901 was photographed leaving Birmingham's Bull Ring bus station to head back to Tamworth, in the heart of 'Mercian' territory. Trevor Follows

LEFT In the Shrewsbury and Ludlow areas the Midland Red fleetname was replaced by 'Hotspur' displayed on a turquoise band. Former Harper Bros Daimler Fleetline/ Northern Counties No 2232 shows the effect as it departs Shrewsbury for Ludlow in August 1983. *Trevor Follows*

BELOW In its early days Midland Red (North) gained a number of Leyland Leopards and Nationals from Midland Red (East), Midland Red (West) and Midland Red (Express), while in 1983 four ex-London Transport Daimler Fleetlines were transferred from Western National. Initially these ran in their previous owner's green livery, on which the 'Chaserider' name, in claret, shows up none too well in this view of Park Royal-bodied No 1916 at Cannock garage in October 1983. The garage here had been opened on 7 February 1977, replacing both Cradley Heath and the ex-Harper premises at Heath Hayes, and, with an initial allocation of 78, had more vehicles than any other MROC garage, as well as being 100% one-man-operated from the outset. *Trevor Follows*

ABOVE Midland Red (North) N8 Leyland National No 694 was painted in a promotional livery to publicise the local 'Tellus' tickets and when photographed in the yard at Wellington garage in February 1984 had not received the violet band associated with area. The destination blind is displaying the garage and the vehicle-type code, which, being for internal company use, would not normally be seen by the public. Trevor Follows

MIDDLE An interesting loan to two of the Midland Red companies involved five MAN/Göppel articulated buses, four of which had started life with South Yorkshire PTE, the fifth having served as a demonstrator before joining the others in Sheffield. In 1982 they moved to the Midlands, initially running on loan to City of Oxford and then to Midland Red (Express) before appearing with Midland Red (West) at Redditch (see page 89), and in January 1984 all five were purchased by Midland Red (North), which allocated them to Cannock. Most were soon repainted poppy red with claret band and 'Chaserider' fleetnames and stag motif, as well as the familiar NBC 'double-N' logo; so treated in June 1984, No 1801 was photographed just outside the town's bus station on 18 August. Destined to be withdrawn in February 1987, this bus would be sold along with three of the others to an operator in Cairns, in Queensland, Australia! Dick White

LEFT Midland Red (North) Leyland Tiger/Plaxton No 1512 looks very smart as it arrives at the Showbus rally at Woburn on 2 September 1984. At this time the Mercian coach unit was based at Tamworth, but just over 18 months later it would transfer to a new depot, opened on 1 April 1986 in Station Road, Lichfield, as the base for a new minibus operation in the city. Dick White

MIDLAND RED (SOUTH)

TOP AND ABOVE With regard to local-identity names Midland Red (South) management pursued a different policy from their counterparts at Midland Red (North), electing to discontinue the use of 'Rugby' and 'Leamington & Warwick' logos from April and May 1982 respectively and the 'Ridercross' name at Banbury from March 1983. Despite this, N2 Leyland National No 287 retained 'Rugby' branding when photographed in its home town in March 1983, while Leamington-based N6 No 584 still displayed the 'Leamington & Warwick' name when recorded on 10 June in Queen Victoria Road, Coventry, en route to the city's Pool Meadow bus station. Trevor Follows, Tom Moore

RIGHT In terms of vehicle policy Midland Red (South) mirrored Midland Red (North), purchasing new Leyland Olympian double-deck buses, Leyland Tiger coaches and large numbers of minibuses. The first batch of Olympians comprised nine ECW-bodied buses delivered in 1983. Three more followed in 1984, along with two which had coach seating, this pair wearing a new dual-purpose livery unique to Midland Red (South). In this photograph the cold is almost palpable as No 960, bound for Leicester on service X67, braves a snowstorm in Corporation Street, Coventry, on 4 January 1986. Tom Moore

LEFT An early-model Leyland National, new in 1973, Midland Red (South) No 102 was one of eight purchased second-hand from Northern General in April 1984 (including two that were for spares only) and was photographed at Leicester's St Margaret's bus station in June of that year. The revised fleetname, applied in standard NBC style, had been introduced in May 1982. Trevor Follows

MIDDLE In February 1985 Midland Red (South) acquired four Northern Counties-bodied Daimler Fleetlines that had been new in 1972 to West Riding. They were numbered 952-5, No 952 being seen at Leamington garage in April 1985. Note the lack of a 'double-N' symbol. Trevor Follows

BELOW LEFT Between December 1984 and November 1985 Midland Red (South) applied a single-deck version of its new dual-purpose livery, which had been introduced on the coach-seated Leyland Olympians, to its 13 SDP28-class Marshall-bodied Leopards. Repainted thus in March 1985, No 332 is seen in Sheffield, helping out on National Express work, on a warm day in June of that year. Mike Greenwood

BELOW RIGHT D13 No 6182 was one of a pair of Midland Red (South) Daimler Fleetlines converted to open-top in 1985, additionally having its centre exit removed at the same time. Renumbered 991 and named Warwick Castle, it is seen working the shuttle between Coventry and the Royal Showground at Stoneleigh on 4 July. The other bus, D12 No 6095, was renumbered 990 and, being also topless, was named more aptly as Lady Godiva! Tom Moore

MIDLAND RED (EAST) - MIDLAND FOX

TOP Following the split Midland Red (East)'s management soon started looking at an alternative livery for the fleet. This early experimental scheme, using poppy red and a rich yellow, was applied to D12 Daimler Fleetline No 6117, dating from 1967. It did not meet with approval, but to avoid the expense of a further repaint the broad expanse of yellow between the decks was used to promote various ticket deals, as seen in this view of the bus making its way out of Leicester along Humberstone Road in March 1982. Midland Red (East) inherited half of Midland Red's remaining Daimler Fleetlines, the oldest of which were 15 years old. Trevor Follows

MIDDLE The new livery chosen by Midland Red (East) was overall red, of a darker shade than that used in BMMO days. Here D13 Daimler Fleetline No 6170, painted in the new colour, heads towards the centre of Leicester in May 1982; note that it still has grey wheels, albeit with red hubs. Trevor Follows

BELOW Not satisfied with introducing a revised bus livery, Midland Red (East) experimented with a number of schemes aimed at injecting a bit more dynamism into the dual-purpose livery. CDP22 Leyland Leopard/ Willowbrook No 797 had received 'Expressway' vinyls promoting the company's long-distance limited-stop services, when photographed at St Margaret's bus station in Leicester in June 1982. Trevor Follows

LEFT Between 1981 and 1983, in order to reduce the average age of its fleet, Midland Red (East) purchased a large number of seven-year-old Daimler/Leyland Fleetlines that had been new to London Transport. These were classified D15 and, having been converted to single-door and repainted at Carlyle Works, were used to replace not only the native D12 Fleetlines but also Leyland Leopards and Nationals. One of seven slightly older examples, of similar origin but acquired in 1982 after a spell as driver-trainers with London Country, Park Royal-bodied No 2654 nevertheless looks smart in the dark-red livery as it leaves Leicester's Sandacre Street garage via the rear exit in July 1983. At this time the garage was still in general use as an NCP car park but was being used temporarily as a coach station. The first two weeks of July constituted Leicester's traditional holiday fortnight, which generated a mass exodus on Saturdays to various seaside towns, and all sorts of vehicles were used to transport the large numbers wishing to travel; note the Derby City Transport Ailsa on the right. One wonders how many passengers would still be smiling after travelling on a DMS all the way to Ingoldmells, some 87 miles distant! Trevor Follows

MIDDLE The first vehicle to appear in the yellow-front livery was Daimler Fleetline/ Metro-Cammell No 2754, so treated in May 1983. Pursued by D12 No 6027, it was photographed at Leicester's St Margaret's bus station in June. The green Bristol VR partially visible on the right belonged to fellow NBC subsidiary Lincolnshire Road Car, which operated a service between Leicester and Grantham. Trevor Follows

LEFT It was widely known that Midland Red (East) was seeking a new trading name (or names) for its operation, and this photograph of D12 No 6099 in the yard at Southgate Street garage in October 1983 suggests that 'Leicester City Division' was one option being considered, although this has proved impossible to corroborate. The bus had been placed in store in July and would be officially withdrawn in November. Trevor Follows

86

RIGHT The first new buses for Midland Red (East) arrived in the autumn of 1983 in the form of a dozen ECW-bodied Leyland Olympians. These wore the company's new livery of yellow and red, initially with small Midland Red fleetnames but minus the NBC symbol. No 4501 was photographed in the small bus station at The Newarke, Leicester. *Trevor Follows*

MIDDLE The new name of 'Midland Fox' was eventually launched on 15 January 1984. Here, in August of that year, Leyland National 2 No 3831 – originally 831 and, as such, numerically the last new bus delivered to MROC – shows off the definitive version of the new livery in Abbey Street, Leicester; by now the old bus station at St Margaret's was being demolished to make way for a new one, and the adjacent Abbey Street was being used on a temporary basis. Note the metal fleet-number plate, introduced earlier in the year. Some Tilling fleets had used such plates for many years, and it was surely no coincidence that the new fleet engineer was an ex-Lincolnshire Road Car man! *Trevor Follows*

BELOW More ex-London Fleetlines arrived in 1984, among them six acquired from Western National in exchange for Leyland Nationals. By the end of the year, however, supplies had dried up, so 10 ECW-bodied Fleetlines, dating from 1972, were acquired from Yorkshire Woollen, entering service in 1985. Awaiting final preparation, Nos 2618 and 2621 are seen parked in the yard adjacent to Southgate Street garage in November 1984. *Trevor Follows*

TOP Resplendent in Midland Fox livery, SDP27 Leyland Leopard/Marshall No 213 basks in the sunshine at Swadlincote bus station in November 1984. Trevor Follows

ABOVE The last major development at Midland Red (East) prior to renaming was the acquisition of N&S Coaches of Market Harborough in December 1983. Supposedly the purchase was completed on the 25th, so perhaps it was a Christmas present for the management team! Eight Plaxton-bodied coaches joined the fleet, these comprising seven Fords and a solitary DAF; formerly the flagship of the N&S fleet, by now numbered 8001 and displaying Midland Fox fleetnames (as well as an NBC badge on the grille), the last-mentioned is seen leaving the new St Margaret's bus station in July 1985. N&S vehicles all displayed names on the rear, and No 8001 was named Lady Diana, although in view of its registration Ray might have been more appropriate. Midland Fox not only retained the names but also proceeded to name some of its own coaches. Trevor Follows

RIGHT In July 1985 Midland Fox received the first of an eventual total of 177 16-seat Ford Transits, all branded 'Fox Cub'. The initial deliveries entered service at Coalville, further minibus services being introduced in Leicester and Hinckley in September. Dormobile-bodied No M90, pictured in somewhat inclement conditions in Scraptoft Lane, Leicester, in February 1987, had entered service in October 1985, in which month the city's Sandacre Street garage (since 1980 used by NCP as a car park) was recommissioned as a bus garage to accommodate the vast influx of minibuses. The first 'Fox Cub' is now preserved and can be seen on display at Snibston Discovery Park, near Coalville. Dick White

RIGHT By the time the Midland Fox image was introduced most of the older, D12 Fleetlines had been replaced, but some of the newer D13s survived long enough to receive the new livery. Seen turning from Charles Street into Rutland Street, in the centre of Leicester, No 6221 was bound for South Wigston when photographed on 21 June 1986. Mike Greenwood

BELOW Making quite a sight on 19 April 1987, a convoy of seven ECW-bodied Leyland Olympians heads along the A6 into Loughborough, with the Woodthorpe turning in the background. Although one of the buses is urging us to 'have a nice day' there is no indication of the final destination, and we can only assume that they were on their way to take up a major private-hire job. Derek Bailey collection

RIGHT A less-well-known derivate of the Midland Fox brand appeared in March 1987, when two Leyland Nationals were outshopped in a 'Midland Wolf' livery. This was a response to a Loughborough–Leicester service that had been introduced by local independent G. K. Kinch, the 'Wolf' vehicles being used on a competing fast service offering cheap fares. Here No 3491 (formerly 491) leaves St Margaret's bus station on 19 May. Trevor Follows

MIDLAND RED (WEST)

LEFT Immediately after the split in September 1981 Midland Red (West) had no double-deckers in its fleet, but later that same month it acquired four Alexander-bodied Daimler Fleetlines – a D12 (No 6043) from Midland Red (South) and three of the four ex-Trent examples that had been the last buses acquired by Midland Red Omnibus Co. One of the latter, No 2545, is seen in Hereford in April 1982. Within three years all the double-deckers had been withdrawn, and the fleet was again 100% single-deck. Trevor Follows

BELOW As outlined earlier (see page 81) Midland Red (West) had five MAN/Göppel articulated buses on loan throughout 1983. At this stage they retained their South Yorkshire PTE fleet numbers and livery, No 2005 (the former demonstrator) being seen operating the busy Matchborough Circular route in October 1983, a couple of months before termination of the loan. Just discernible on the side are two small 'Reddibus' fleetnames (one on each section of the bus), produced specifically to match the non-standard livery. Stuart Turner

TOP In April 1983 Midland Red (West) took over the Hereford city routes operated latterly by G. H. Yeomans, as well as the latter's Hereford–Credenhill service, hiring and, later, acquiring two of its Duple-bodied Bedford YMTs for use thereon. Initially these retained full Yeomans livery, but in May 1984 they had their one-man fare equipment removed and were repainted in white coach livery, in which No 846 is seen at Worcester in June of that year. *Trevor Follows*

ABOVE The Midland Red (West) fleet remained fairly stable in the first few years, seeing just a handful of acquisitions from other Midland Red companies. The first new vehicle, a 50-seat Plaxton-bodied Leyland Tiger coach, arrived in 1983; numbered 1001, it was given the distinctive registration FEH 1Y issued by Stoke-on-Trent LVLO, obtaining a '1' registration having proven impossible at Worcester. Wearing the latest National Express livery style of white with red and blue 'venetian blind' stripes but with the company's own fleetname, it was photographed at Keele Services on the M6 in October 1983. *Trevor Follows*

ABOVE From 1985 Midland Red (West)'s excursions and private hires were marketed under the 'MidWest' name, coaches being painted in an attractive livery of white, maroon and gold. Among these was Leyland Leopard/Plaxton No 1031, a rebody of CDP22 No 804 of 1980, its original Willowbrook body having been badly damaged in an accident. In December 1985 it was parked in the rather muddy yard adjacent to Worcester's Padmore Street garage. Trevor Follows

MIDDLE On 23 November 1985 Midland Red (West) launched a new network of services in Worcester, using a fleet of 59 Mercedes-Benz L608D minibuses. The fleetname 'Citibus' was used, accompanied on the sides by the City of Worcester coat of arms. No 1308 was one of 19 with 20-seat PMT body conversions, the other 40 having been similarly converted by Robin Hood. A further 45 Mercedes-Benz minibuses would be purchased in 1986, these having body conversions by Alexander (one), Robin Hood (21) and Reeve Burgess (23). Trevor Follows

LEFT A striking new livery was introduced by Midland Red (West) in 1986, shortly before the company was privatised. Most vehicles, however, received it after the management buy-out, such being the case with Leyland National No 256. It is seen in a rather damp Worcester bus station, having arrived from Birmingham on the 144 service, in October 1987. Trevor Follows

MIDLAND EXPRESS

TOP Midland Express was a joint venture between the four bus-operating Midland Red companies, which showed varying degrees of enthusiasm for the concept. Midland Red (North)'s vehicular contribution included a selection of older Leyland Leopards but also seven new Duple-bodied Leyland Tigers that entered service in 1984, among them No 1601, pictured at Wellington in March 1985. The 'venetian blind' stripes serve as a reminder that NBC's corporate image, although increasingly relaxed, still held sway in most areas at this time. Trevor Follows

ABOVE Also delivered to Midland Red (North) in 1984 were three Leyland Olympians with 70-seat dual-purpose ECW bodywork, these too entering service in Midland Express livery. No 1913 negotiates Birmingham's Bull Ring in April 1985 on its regular X31 route, which linked the city with towns and villages in the area around Cannock Chase, befitting the Chaserider fleetname. Tom Moore

ABOVE Midland Red (South) painted just six vehicles in Midland Express livery, all of them Leyland Leopards; one had Plaxton coachwork, the other five Willowbrook. They were so treated in 1983 but did not last long in this condition, all having reverted to white coach livery by April 1985. Here, in August 1983, Willowbrook-bodied No 802 has attracted a goodly number of passengers at Stratford-upon-Avon bus station; partially visible in the background is the former Stratford Blue garage. Tom Moore

MIDDLE Midland Red (East) – Midland Fox from January 1984 – fully embraced the Midland Express concept, continuing to use the name for many years. Willowbrook-bodied Leyland Leopard No 797 had received an experimental 'Expressway' livery (see page 84) and, indeed, several other trial schemes prior to the launch of the Midland Express brand. By August 1984 it had gained the new colours and is seen here near Stoneleigh while making its way, at some speed, from Leicester to Stratford. Dick White

LEFT Eight 47-seat Willowbrook Spacecar-bodied Leyland Leopards dating from 1977 were purchased by Midland Red (East) from National Travel (West) in 1983, and these were numbered 50-7. All received Midland Express livery, No 54 being seen so adorned in Leicester's High Street in March 1984; although suitable for long-distance motorway work it was on this occasion operating a local bus service. Partially visible on the left, heading out of the city, is sister vehicle No 56. Dick White

RIGHT Midland Fox also applied Midland Express livery to some older dual-purpose Leopards inherited from Midland Red Omnibus Co and to four ex-West Riding examples with attractive Alexander 49-seat Y-type bodywork. Dating from 1975, these latter were purchased in May 1985 and repainted in June and July. No 380 was photographed in Gravel Street, Leicester, adjacent to St Margaret's bus station, in July 1985. Trevor Follows

MIDDLE Midland Red (West) treated a large number of Leopard/Plaxton grant coaches to Midland Express livery, among them CDP20 No 732, seen leaving Worcester for Great Malvern in June 1985. The company would perpetuate the brand after privatisation, albeit with a simplified livery application. Dick White

BELOW The only new Leyland Nationals to be received after the split were six Gardner-engined National 2s – to 'Suburban Coach' specification, with 47 high-backed seats and luggage racks – delivered to Midland Red (West) in the spring of 1984. They entered service in Midland Express livery, No 1204 being seen thus at Worcester bus station on 3 June 1985; note also the electronic destination display with which these vehicles were fitted. In 1986 a number of Redditch-based N4s would be similarly painted, although this was a purely cosmetic exercise, the vehicles in question retaining their standard bus seating. Dick White

ABOVE And finally ... a last look at Midland Red in the early days of the corporate era. Viewed from an elevated vantage-point on 15 June 1974, Leicester's St Margaret's bus station is filled with a wide variety of Midland Red buses, all smartly turned out in NBC poppy red. Mike Greenwood

Bibliography

Midland Red has always attracted the interest of enthusiasts, and the following books, which were used for research in the production of this volume, will provide much interesting material for readers who wish to follow up this subject.

Glory Days: Midland Red by Mike Greenwood (Ian Allan, 1998)
Harpers Bus Memories in Colour by Paul Roberts
    (Irwell Press, 2012)
The Heyday of Midland Red by Mike Greenwood & Malcolm
    Keeley (Ian Allan, 2005)
Independent Buses in Shropshire by Neville Mercer
    (Venture Publications, 2011)
Independent Buses in Staffordshire by Neville Mercer
    (Venture Publications 2009)
The Leyland National by Paul Chancellor
    (Trans-Pennine Publishing, 2007)
Midland Red Buses by M. W. Greenwood (Bradford Barton, 1980)
Midland Red Bus Garages by Malcolm Keeley (Ian Allan, 2013)
Midland Red Volume 2: A History of the company and its
    vehicles from 1940 to 1970 by Paul Gray, Malcolm Keeley
    and John Seale (Transport Publishing Co, 1979)
Midland Red Motorway Coaches by Steve Richards
    (Richards Publishing, 2012)
Midland Red – the Transitional Years by Les Simpson
    (Trans-Pennine Publishing, 2008)
Midland Red North by Neil MacDonald
    (Venture Publications, 1995)
Midland Red Style by Roger Torode and Malcolm Keeley
    (Capital Transport, 2011)
Midlands Bus Memories in Colour by Paul Roberts
    (Irwell Press, 2007)
More room on Top – the BMMO D9 and D10 by Steve Richards
    (Richards Publishing, 2012)
National Bus Company 1968-1989 by John Birks et al
    (Transport Publishing Co, 1990)
National Bus Company – the Early Years by Kevin Lane
    (Ian Allan, 2004)
National Bus Company – the Road to Privatisation
    by Kevin Lane (Ian Allan, 2006)
West Midlands by Malcolm Keeley (Capital Transport, 1988)
West Midlands PTE Buses and Trolleybuses by Malcolm Keeley
    (Ian Allan, 2009)
Working Days: Midland Red by Malcolm Keeley
    (Ian Allan, 2008)

Other publications consulted and likely to be of additional interest to readers include various issues of Buses magazine covering the NBC era, PSV Circle News Sheets covering the years 1968-88, PSV Circle Fleet Histories of Midland Red (North), Midland Red (South) and Midland Red (West), published in 1991, 1993 and 1991 respectively, Midland Red 'Staff Bulletins' dating from the period 1968-72 and official fleet lists produced by Midland Red and West Midlands PTE in 1975, along with various timetables issued by both operators.

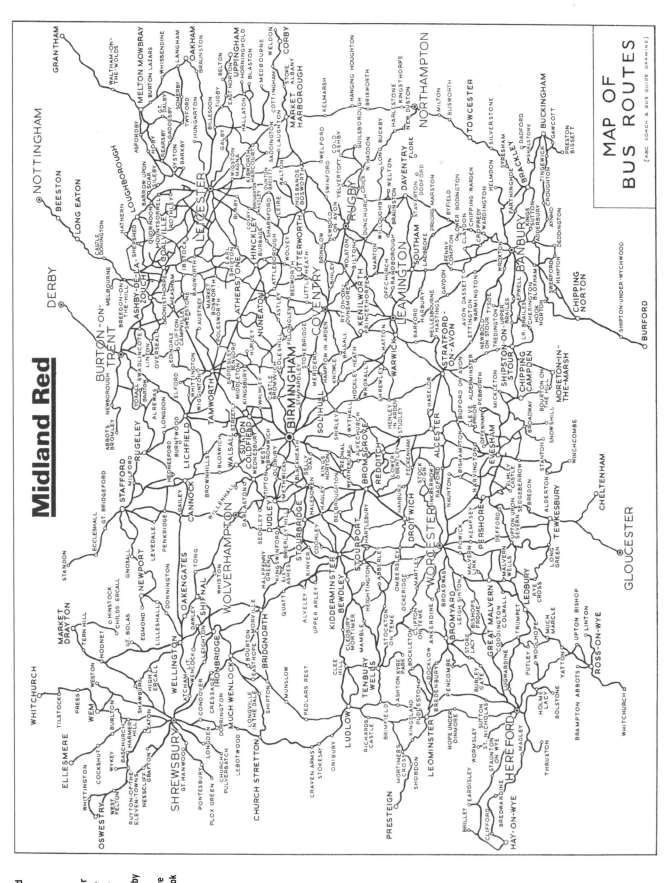

Midland Red

MAP OF BUS ROUTES

[ABC COACH & BUS GUIDE DRAWING]

RIGHT The Midland Red 'Map of Bus Routes' that was issued in the summer of 1969. It would be another three years before the NBC corporate identity became all-pervasive, and by then the route network would have a very different look to it.